This book is dedicated to the legions of empty-nesters, whose children have packed their bags and headed off to explore life in far-flung towns, cities or countries.

Now is the time to pack your bags and set out to enjoy your own adventure – whether you journey near or far, just do something different, push boundaries, scoop up some memories and have fun.

Bon Voyage.

Contents

Preface

A quick explanation about the people, places and facts mentioned in this book, to ensure that I am not making inadvertent or inappropriate misrepresentations. The named characters exist and only on one occasion have I changed an individual's name, as I did not want to incur the wrath of a Western Australian policeman for a second time.

Although the places I visited are well recognised and well documented some of the facts might seem a little obscure. I have endeavoured to double-check that my original jottings were correct but if errors have been made, then I take full responsibility and will amend as and when identified, on the rather presumptuous assumption that this book might run to a re-print.

I should perhaps point out that my travels took place approximately fourteen years before I finally converted my handwritten scrawl into something more legible. In the intervening years, hotels have been given face-lifts and the smaller museums have embraced the 21st-century technology of their larger cousins, so my occasional disparaging remarks no longer apply. I am also certain that it is possible to do what I did on a more nutritious diet than the beer and muffin fest which fuelled my adventures and expanded my girth.

Finally, and weirdly, I must thank people who may never be aware that I have written about them, which is such a pity as without their conversations this publication would be merely pamphlet sized.

Where to begin?

I am not someone normally given to scribbling down life's events, as keeping a diary requires a discipline I sadly lack. Instead, I airily commit moments to memory where they tumble around, resurfacing unbidden in a day-dream inducing fog. Well, that was the norm until a few years ago when this random approach to memory recall changed out of necessity.

In 2000, buoyed up by the enthusiastic global welcome given to the new millennium, my son Matt decided that a belated gap year would be a good idea. Before I could mumble parental words of pecuniary caution, both he and his girlfriend, Alice, had quit their jobs to set off on an around-the-world trip. As two sets of teary parents bid farewell to their offspring, Alice's fatalistic father muttered, "They won't be back." Strangely I hadn't considered that option, so my adamant, "Yes, they will," probably sounded a little naïve.

Six months later the back-packing duo arrived in Sydney where, predictably, they ran out of money and, unpredictably, they found work. Friends were made, a lifestyle enjoyed and then marriage, Australian citizenship, three gorgeous daughters and a mortgage swiftly followed. Alice's father was right. Sydney had become home and I miss them with a maternal and grand-maternal ache. To add to my woes, at about the same time that Matt flew off to the unknown his sister, Kate, a primary school teacher, decided to work overseas. Another teary farewell at Heathrow followed. Sadly, the nest had emptied all too swiftly.

And then to compound this strange feeling of loss, in 2002 the disability charity I had been working for ceased to exist. Suddenly, I was minus a job and minus motivation. Trying to shift me out of this lumpen inertia my husband, Kevin, suggested that a trip to Sydney might cheer me up. What a boost! I think possibly he had a three-week visit in mind, but I started chatting to a friendly chap at Trailfinders and my itinerary just got longer and longer. The planning was fun and I ignored friends' questions about how many home-cooked frozen meals I was going to leave for my beloved: none as it turned out.

Finally, with preparations over and bag neatly packed, I was gleefully on my way, off on my first solo adventure. In a little under seven weeks I hopped from London to Los Angeles, down to the Cook Islands, further down to North Island, New Zealand before heading across the Tasman Sea to Australia. As adventures go, it wasn't the most intrepid of expeditions for, without giving the game away, there were no *Shirley Valentine* moments and nothing went wrong.

Eighteen months after my return, with a barely resuscitated piggybank cowering nervously in the corner, I decided upon a further frenzied shake of its rattling innards. The travel bug had bitten deep but further excuses of inertia seemed implausible, so I focussed on the fact that there were still dots on the Australian landscape waiting to be joined up. Once again, aided and abetted by the helpful staff at Trailfinders, my itinerary grew and grew.

On both of these trips, the only obligation I was placed under by my patient husband, was that I should not rely on my jumbled memory to regale him with my antics, but instead write a daily travel journal, which I duly did – albeit in a 50 pence lined exercise book.

Oh, and by the way, George was my green wheelie suitcase.

I was on my way

Twenty-four hours in California

Friday 22nd March: Ready for the off – did I wave goodbye at London Heathrow?

There was no last embrace. No entreaty to keep safe – from either party. Perhaps I waved? I couldn't be sure. I was too busy inhaling fumes. Glassy-eyed I drew in that wonderful heady cocktail of aircraft fuel. Forget fresh-baked bread, for me it's the whiff of kerosene which guarantees a satisfied *aah* will escape my lips. Excitement bubbled with each breath. Childhood tales of pilots who, with derring-do, re-lived their RAF days bouncing passenger planes safely onto grassy runways, had obviously nurtured this olfactory addiction. Inhaling happily, I hefted my bag and hopefully waved a cheery goodbye to my nearest and dearest. Skipping off, I mused that anything forgotten could be acquired as and when – I wasn't exactly heading into a wilderness. A final "Don't forget to write" drifted across the buzz of airline activity, acknowledged by my barely considered, "Yeah – byee." I was on my way.

But before I had made it through passport control, I was halted in my tracks by revised stringent security measures and my little bubble of excitement went 'pop'. With an unwelcome feeling of fluster, I felt the impact of the searches before being allowed to weigh George, my pristine suitcase. For some random reason, together with half a dozen other bods, all blokes, I was singled out for special treatment. Trying not to look crestfallen, I surreptitiously surveyed the aged twenty-something backpackers beside me and silently questioned: *Why middle-aged me*?

Fluster upon fluster, the extra screening involved quickly unpacking the carefully packed contents of George, to display underwear and toiletries to all and sundry. With horror, I watched as individual tampons skittered across the heavily peopled floor, adding an extra challenge to the peripatetic navigations of bemused passengers. For some unknown reason I had thought it clever to take the offending items from their box and stuff handfuls into the nooks and crannies of the case: daft idea, never again. Grovelling on my knees, I scooped up the escapees and re-stashed everything clumsily and hurriedly. Red-faced I plonked the case on the scales, refusing to engage in eye contact with anyone in a uniform. This fraught pantomime and unexpected exercise cut short the pre-flight waiting time, which meant that my duty-free spree was reduced to a quick sprint for a bottle of Dior perfume, my one luxury item, plus an attractive flesh-coloured money belt: *Whose flesh I wonder*?

Arriving at the departure gate we the marked few, and I do mean that literally as a quick squint at the passenger manifest revealed that the naughty names had been marked in bright pink highlighter with a couple of yellow asterisks alongside, again received special treatment. This time our shoes had to be thoroughly inspected, requiring a certain amount of grunting on my part as I struggled with the stiff laces of my new trainers. Strangely, I had never possessed a pair of trainers before setting off on this trip. By now I was getting sweatier by the minute. I'm a seasoned traveller but had never experienced such heat-inducing scrutiny.

Returning from a pre-adventure shoe-shopping expedition,

my husband had queried my (for me) odd choice of footwear in a way which signalled a possible wobble in case his wife's mid-life crisis might extend to more radical departures than just shoe choice. Looking down at my now sock-clad feet I wondered if he had been right, should I have kept to my sensible Mary Jane's? *Had my feet singled me out?*

The only reason for going on about this at any length is because of the frosty raised eyebrow (a single eyebrow being more humiliating) reception I received when I eventually sauntered on board, admittedly appearing a little more bedraggled than I had three hours previously. It might have been my imagination working overtime or pure paranoia at play, but I am sure that the silent message conveyed by the pink highlight and brace of yellow stars had preceded me onto the flight. Magically the first gin and tonic thawed my rictus jaw but alas no crew member reciprocated with growing warmth.

Had my feet singled me out?

Happily, apart from one minor blip, the flight was uneventful which, as we landed, I hoped the remaining twelve would likewise be. The blip occurred when the only air turbulence we hit was timed to coincide with my decision to disturb 19B to get to the loo. Having woken him once, as I climbed out from my window seat, becoming entangled in his hair-raising static-crackling blanket, I then had to turn and clamber back over him when, on cue, the 'fasten seat belt' sign was illuminated. He didn't budge, only grunting in a non-committal sort of way.

It's weirdly unsettling engaging in such close physical contact with an inert unknown individual. Inevitably, I had to wake him for a second time when, twenty minutes later, stratospheric calm was restored. Apologetically scrambling over his bulk to resume my progress towards the loo, his grunts were now of a more annoyed kind. Earlier I had become acquainted with19B by attaching half of his seat belt to half of mine. When he pointed out my error, it explained the lump pressing into my right buttock, the unused portion of my seat belt. *Did I say I was a seasoned traveller?*

Touchdown in Los Angeles came punctually and smoothly and my welcome in the city of the angels by airport officials was warm and friendly. No longer was I a travelling pariah. Reunited with George, I soon found myself in a taxi lurching towards Santa Monica. From memory, the roads in New England, my only other experience of American roads, couldn't compete with these racetracks: scary stuff. After much lane changing and Spanish invective, we arrived at Four Points, a rather weary looking Sheraton Hotel but ideally situated just ten minutes walk from the famous Santa Monica Boulevard and Muscle Beach.

During the madcap taxi ride, I admit to a certain feeling of flatness. I'm not sure what I was expecting, but the chosen route from the airport to Santa Monica was lined with tired, shabby buildings and it seemed that most of the population was equally tired and shabby and in need of a hot meal and a hot bath. I don't recall seeing so many supermarket trolley homes in a comparable distance in London. En route from the airport, the roseate hue that had quivered over the California of my dreams looked a little tarnished in the tawdry reality of four in the afternoon.

Having arrived at my first destination, dragging the unexpected excess baggage of feeling jaded, my bed beckoned only to be swiftly rebuffed; this was no time for being a wimp.

With just a day in the US of A prior to catching the next flight, I opted for a quick wash and brush-up before stepping out onto Pico Boulevard and then heading down the hill in search of the sea. And when I found it… Wow. What a view. Fabulous!

The sea seemingly merged into the sky creating a magical wrap-around feel and a truly fantastic palm-framed vista opened up in front of me. Beaming happily whilst standing on the edge of the sand, digging in my shoe-clad toes, I watched as the Pacific rolled gently out towards the setting sun. The sea absorbed and mirrored the sun's golden glow as it gently spread over the clouds that were sitting puffed and fluffy on the distant horizon. It was difficult to tell the point at which the golden sea became the golden sky. Any remnants of the jaded traveller swiftly vanished at this point. The adventure had truly begun.

All the things I had been expecting to find along the boulevard, I now found. Skateboarders, cyclists and roller bladers scrunched rhythmically on the sand encrusted path. One energetic male, not very muscle-bound, and several less energetic females, not overly clad, showed off their varying degrees of athletic prowess on the rings, parallel bars and more besides, which appear to grow up out of the sand. So this was the famed Muscle Beach. *But where were the six-pack hunks?*

Just behind, on the other side of the path and under the shade of the palms, were the permanent chess board tables I'd seen in glossy magazines. Assorted characters sat in deep contemplation, possibly over the next move, but in the mellow light of the dusk it could have been over anything. This was sunset on, what seemed to me, a watery sandy haven. Strolling back up the hill to the hotel, redistributing particles of Muscle Beach with each stride, I was again struck by the alien feel of the environment and realised that it was not a place for walkers. Crossing roads was a challenge. *Where were the pedestrian lights?* If and when they did exist they lured you confidently out into the road where, at the midway point, they suddenly favoured the motorist and you knew you should have sprinted... 'cos you're suddenly an unwitting participant in a heart-pumping game of chicken played by some very big cars.

By now it was about six in the evening and my body clock was beginning to protest, but, deciding to delay bedtime a little longer, I stopped at the hotel bar for a cold beer. Refreshing though the bevy was, it soon induced a greater feeling of tiredness. Fearful of sleeping now and then waking up raring to go at two in the morning, I struggled on, yawning attractively, wondering who had designed the hotel décor and what overall effect they had been trying to achieve. A rather strange mock-coal fire, complete with classical over mantel, might have added a homely touch, but for its position. Marooned in a terrazzo sea it looked surreal with its truncated chimneybreast pointing up into nothingness. It was as if someone had cleaved it from the wall of a mansion and plonked it at a jaunty angle in the hotel lobby, whilst deciding where to give it a permanent home. *Perhaps the house wrecker was one of my drinking companions?*

Anyway, done with being picky about my surroundings, I ambled off to find my room which was, as ever when I'm on my own, located a route march from anywhere. Possibly the biggest bug-bear of being a lone female traveller is the room allocation lottery: I rarely win. In the UK I used to think I was indelibly marked with the stamp of charity worker (pauper) or leper (unclean) by the way the least attractive and most secluded rooms were always reserved for me. Had my reputation preceded me across the Atlantic? Perhaps there was more to that pink highlighter and those yellow asterisks? Here I was, on the ninth of nine floors at the furthest point from the lift, down a twisty corridor with *bingo* a service-lift-shaft to keep me company.

After a bit of pottering and conversing with home to get my mobile phone operational, I ordered room service – burger and fries – well, this was America. The food arrived promptly and cheerily, the service lift proving to be an unexpected bonus. Greedily I tucked into a delicious burger with piping hot chips and another cold beer as *Frasier* hit the screen. Total bliss. No sooner than I'd licked the last dribble of grease from my fingers when curtains fell.

I slept soundly, undisturbed by buzzing brain or garrulous guests, and awoke at a sensible time with the Getty Center as my mission.

Saturday 23rd March: and the reason for my twenty-four hours in California

Packed and ready to go by ten o'clock, with George safely secreted in the baggage room, the doorman directed me to the Number 7 bus stop. As a parting shot, he added that I'd have to change to a Number 14 at Brondy to get to my destination. Studying my newly acquired timetable it seemed that a bus was due and, as I headed up the hill, sure enough I heard the rumble of the Big Blue Bus. I ran for the stop.

Clambering aboard, an unexpectedly jovial driver greeted me with, "Hey, that was a bus run, if ever I saw one."

"Yes – phew," I panted, "I'm off to the Getty Center."

"Not on this bus, you're not," came his too jolly reply, "you want a 7 not a 3."

Almost before a small disappointed squeak escaped my lips he added, "Not to worry – I'll take you to the next stop – where're you from?"

"London."

"London – well great – here's a ticket that'll see you to the Getty."

"London," echoed the old wino lurching in the gangway, "that's great."

With the next bus stop upon us, the doors wheezed open

and I climbed down the precipitous steps to chimes of "Have a nice day" from the driver, the wino and the rest of passengers. I turned, gave a regal British wave and blushed scarlet. The driver had given me a bus ticket, free of charge, and suddenly I felt ten feet tall and was probably grinning broadly.

Transfer from 3 to 7 to 14 completed, I found myself at the Getty, just as the clouds rolled in over what had started out as a 'nice day'. The temperature dropped dramatically. Okay, we were considerably higher than sea level up in the foothills of the Santa Monica Mountains, where my *I'm on my holidays* clothing suddenly seemed to be lacking a layer or two. Having decided to carry all my worldly goods in a money belt, I discovered a further use for this sartorially attractive accessory – it doubled as a tummy warmer.

An electric train takes visitors up to the museum from the car park, and it's all so clean and efficient. Finally arriving at the limestone clad forecourt and entrance the sheer size, views, setting, architecture, everything, takes your breath away. And as I stood gawping, breathless, at all this majesty I became aware of an irate tourist flapping his arms at me. It took me a second or two to compute his actions; I was standing four-square and open-mouthed in his shot. Anyway, once inside, to reduce a day to a word, the contents were 'awesome'.

The Getty is out of this world, both inside and out. Paintings, sculpture, tapestries and illuminated manuscripts plus entire rooms furnished in an array of period settings complete with panelling, peer glasses, commodes, porcelain and on and on. The paintings were top notch, nothing second-rate adorned the walls. I drifted past the finest examples of works by the European masters and had I taken a roll-call, all would have been present and correct. Getty, his family and trustees had obviously bought wisely, but with such a deep purse, it possibly made the shopping easier than for the money conscious national galleries dotted around the globe.

Hard to say what the highlights were, even the building and grounds were stars in their own right. However, there was a temporary exhibition which I found particularly absorbing, as it detailed the restoration of a Roman statue of Emperor Marcus Aurelius with the newly restored Marcus standing proudly in the middle of the room. It was fascinating learning how he'd been put together in the first place, re-pieced and repaired over the centuries as bits dropped off, got broken, or lost, and how it had been restored to enable it to be disassembled at will, boxed up and sent on tour without further damage being caused. Not sure why I found it so absorbing, but it was a fine statue and an incredible jigsaw.

Having admired a Roman statue, it followed that I should inspect the array of Roman artefacts. There were pots and jars used by the proletariat, to which I gave a cursory glance, but this was Los Angeles so I homed in on the bling of the patricians and was not disappointed. Spell-bound before one display cabinet, my eyes locked on to the centrally positioned exhibit, a golden diadem shining like a beacon. The craftsmanship was exquisite and for all its age the headdress, which had once adorned the statue of a goddess, looked both new and at home in its modern-day setting. Regretting my ignorance, I had no idea that such intricate work dated back to… h'm… well a long time ago. Note to self: when keeping a journal, have pen and paper handy at all times.

The Getty grounds were as impressive as the exhibits. Momentarily warmed by a lunch of soup eaten whilst huddled in a sheltered corner of a vast terrace, I wandered amongst bougainvillea, sauntered over springy grass and was wowed by the view. Here I was standing outside the magnificent white buildings set high on the distant hills which could be spotted from my hotel room. Suddenly the chill returned and after a quick foray into the obligatory gift shop, it was time to retrace my steps, via the Big Blue Bus, to the hotel. Sitting at the various bus stops along the route proved as fascinating as the Getty.

Here, all the Spanish speaking world and his wife paraded before me, declaiming with such fervent intensity that it seemed as if speech was soon to be banned, so let's make the most of it. In future, sitting at an English bus stop will feel a tad tame by comparison.

Arriving back at the hotel at four-thirty elated if a trifle weary, and with an hour to spare before catching an airport minibus back to the airport for half the cost of the taxi fare, I decided to end my stay in the way that it had started, by propping up the bar. Perching on a bar stool, I overheard the barmaid say to a group of relaxing air crew that Delta flight crew were her favourite flight crew, United flight attendants her favourite attendants and BA crew were just good fun (they obviously save their sense of humour for when they're on terra firma away from their human cargo).

"That's diplomatic," quipped I.

"Well that's a British accent if ever I heard one," observed a Delta pilot.

"Where're you from?"

"London."

"London!" came the now anticipated chorus.

"Drinks on the house," chirruped the barmaid with cheery largesse.

So, Santa Monica had treated me to a 50 cents bus ride and a free beer. What a start to my adventure.

Warming to the friendliness of the Californian community, with a slight pang of regret I said "goodbye" to my new friends and reclaimed George. Together we set off for the airport just as the evening sky put on another spectacular sunset. My stay might have been brief, but everything had conspired to make sure, in the nicest possible way, that I enjoyed every moment and could forget nothing. My decision to fly west towards Australia had been the right one. Sitting back on the well-worn shuttle bus seat, my thoughts went into their usual pictorial jumble, until the red Californian sky beckoned just as it had done twenty-four hours previously.

"You can thank the pollution for that display," drawled a rather laconic airport bus driver who, with a busload of tourists anxious to catch their flights, made a detour to deposit a heavily laden domestic somewhere near the back of beyond. Whilst she was thrilled with this unexpected act of chivalry, our combined tourist pulses quickened as one, as the minute hand lurched rapidly forward, towards our ever-closer departure times.

Back on track, and as the airport loomed large, I realised that the 'slightly tarnished view' of the Los Angeles of my arrival had been replaced with a view as genuinely rosy as the sunset. The urban sprawl that had seemed so flimsy and unimaginative when I arrived was, I remembered, built on the San Andreas Fault. Function and not form were what mattered most and the people I met during my brief visit had provided the ornamentation and embellishments – with gusto.

Three weeks later and finally in Australia, I wrote the following in a round robin to family and friends at home:

Well here I am in Adelaide at the mid-way point of my adventure. Feel as if I've been on the road for months. Am loving the nomadic lifestyle – perhaps not exactly in the backpacking league, but adventurous enough for someone unused to exploring the unknown. My day wandering around the Getty seems to have happened in another lifetime. Have finally had several rolls of film developed and it was lovely to be reminded of the museum's incredible architecture and its accessibility. Even my 'point and shoot' camera captured the magnificence of the buildings: a place to revisit if I'm ever again allowed a travel pass.

The Cook Islands

Sunday 24th March: goodbye to the USA and hello to a Rarotongan Paradise

Check in at Los Angeles airport was pleasantly uneventful after my London experience followed by a similarly uneventful flight of nine hours fifteen minutes before touch-down at Rarotonga, the largest of the fifteen Cook Islands. As soon as the aircraft door opened, I was reeling drunkenly from my first heady whiff of warm tropical air. The tourist blurb invitingly announced that this was the place to 'awake refreshed, walk along the beach hand in hand... and thrill to the dawn of a new day in Paradise'. Pure hedonistic bliss and as I was about to step into this little piece of paradise, the owner of the hand that I might have held was several thousand miles away tucked up in bed with a bad case of 'flu. *Did I feel guilty?* Well, I like to think so...

Still cheerfully unaware of the 'flu misery back at home, what a fun 'dawn of a new day' island arrival I experienced: a chap singing a melodic welcome, sweetly perfumed frangipani leis draped over the necks of all in-bound passengers and utter confusion as those holiday reps who had managed to crawl, yawning, to the airport for four in the morning tried to recognise their guests, whilst other guests (me included) searched in vain for their still sleeping welcoming party. Finally the confusion melted away and we all, I think, climbed onto the right buses/coaches or vans and fanned out in either a clockwise or anti-clockwise procession around the island. My hotel, the Rarotongan Beach Resort, must be at about six o'clock if the airport is at twelve. Then at 5.37 on Sunday morning, with a welcoming fruit punch drink inside me, and wilting flowers around my neck, I found my way to room 537. *Who orchestrated that?*

As I stepped into my room a genuine squeak of *wow* escaped my lips. Forget my earlier negative remarks about room allocation lotteries, I had just won the jackpot! Surveying my domain this, I thought, was perfect for a girl on her own: lucky me. Masses of space, a king-size bed, a huge bathroom and a balcony shaded by palm trees with ripe papaya tantalisingly within arms reach. It only seemed right to share my joy. However, after several abortive attempts at phoning home, I finally succeeded only to then conduct a monosyllabic conversation. Looking back, perhaps jet lag and sleep depravation played demon tricks whilst 'flu can't have helped the dialogue flow either. Shamefully, I must have sounded very nonplussed about being on a lush tropical island in the middle of the Pacific, especially to someone bed-bound in chilly England.

Signing-off, I flopped spread-eagled onto the bed with no one to nudge me if I snored. After a couple of hours of dreamless snoozing, the clanging of chambermaids aroused me. Up and down the corridor, the strategically placed 'Do not disturb' signs seemed to present a house-keeping challenge as chamber maids persisted with rhythmic door hammering until bleary-eyed holiday makers emerged blinking blankly into the bright sunlight: me included.

Quite right too! Why travel half way around the world just

to sleep? So it was up, shower (with soothing, soft palm soap) and off to the beach where sun, sea and snorkel awaited. And what a fabulous beach... *ouch*, the sand was a bit hot. I felt as if I was tip-toeing over countless teeny burning prisms.

The hotel sits on a slight promontory. On either side, sparkling white arcs of pristine beach combine to form a complete curve around the bay. No other buildings mar the view. Here is a picture postcard come to life: shimmering white sand, shady palm trees, sparkling turquoise water, a frill of breakers out on the horizon and blue, blue skies. Pinch me! I opted for the bit of beach in front of the main bar area and, lily white, waddled into the sea. The water was shallow, surprisingly cool, but ideal for snorkelling. Proving my expertise at this sport and as a de-misting exercise, I spat on the glass of my lovely lime-green mask and clamped the matching snorkel firmly between my teeth. These accessories were a holiday gift from Kate. Handing them over, she had explained that the eye-catching colour was important, as you want people to know that a human-being is attached to the stick poking out of the water. I thought she'd have been proud of the image now created by her properly equipped mother.

The coral came as a surprise, as it looked more dead than alive, but was in fact flourishing. Grey coral of different shapes and sizes with splashes of pinks, purples and yellows, form a protective ring around the bay, keeping sharks out and providing a safe haven for the dozens of varieties of fish and sea slugs and of course the nosey humans. Angel fish, parrot fish, wrasses – in fact a whirl of yellow, black and silver stripes flashed busily past. Initially, I had no idea what I was looking at, but loved flapping around watching the hustle and bustle of fin city through the picture window of my mask. As I looked out someone looked in, it was an almost invisible silver fish which was surprisingly large and I hadn't noticed him until we were both mouthing *eek* eyeball to eyeball.

So typical of me, the lack of breakfast interrupted this watery idyll as hunger pangs began to gnaw at my innards, ending my first dip in the Pacific. By now it was about two-thirty in the afternoon and a toasted cheese and tomato sandwich provided the ideal rumbling-tum filler. Not exactly traditional Cook Islands fare, but very welcome nevertheless. I was not alone in thinking it welcome. Lined up on every hard surface in front of me and looking like a menacing sequence from *The Birds*, sat the island's noisy, jostling bovver boys – rooks/ravens the universal corvid crew. They are not attractive specimens of the bird world and sitting with their beaks open to cool down, increased the scavenging effect. Lunchtime heralded the first of many rain showers; short sharp and not really a problem. What I had missed, or missed most of, whilst head down inspecting the coral community, were the uplifting harmonies of a church choir. Mau Mau'd mamas, papas in bright shirts and radiant sons and daughters in very little, sashayed their way gracefully through their Polynesian Gospel repertoire, for the benefit of a highly appreciative pool-side audience. Of course, today was Sunday.

My absence from the beach was further extended when I spoke to a couple from Derbyshire who had left their seventeen and fifteen year old son and daughter at home and were experiencing the first feelings of mild panic as they'd been unable to reach them on the phone. Anyway, after a longish chat and a poor attempt at consoling them, it was back to the beach for some more splashing around. And then, as the sun began to sink, so did I – not literally, but my energy levels took a dip. The hope that a cool shower would revive me was a hope in vain. When faced with the choice of putting on evening togs or sleeping togs, sleeping won and it was bedtime by seven-thirty. Again, spread-eagled, I drifted off happily undisturbed.

Monday 25th March: time for cafés, communications and curry

A Monday with a difference: no struggling with the beginning of the week London Underground chaos, instead a leisurely breakfast of luscious fresh tropical fruit overlooking the sea followed by the ten-thirty clockwise bus into town. Rarotonga's capital, Avarua, stretches along a fifteen minute amble of the island's coastal road. There is only one further road and it runs behind the coastal road, about 500m inshore although it doesn't encircle the entire island. These are the only roads, so if attempting to go north/south or east/west across the middle, the only way is up and over the mountain... on foot.

My first task in Avarua was to track down a baggy t-shirt for swimming in and a sunhat as I was already lobster-red and that was after liberal slatherings of factor 15 sun-screen. The main shop, Cook Island Trading Company (CITC), is an Aladdin's cave with everything you could want or need, except for cotton t-shirts without football slogans/motifs. Anyway, a reviving smoothie next door meant that I was able to continue a little longer with my quest. Avarua straggles along the road for about three quarters of a mile with the sea on one side and volcanic cones providing a verdant backdrop on the other. Lush green vegetation abounds, softening the structures that are homes, shops, churches, assorted government departments and the Post Office.

Seeing internet prices advertised way below the hotel charges, I spent a happy ten New Zealand dollars worth of messaging. My message home went something like this which probably left the house-bound ailing recipient mutterings things about a spoilt child:

Hi! Sun's shining and I'm in the cool of an internet café feeling oh, so cool myself. So I've made it – to Rarotonga at least. Everything fantastic! I can recommend this spot for a dose of sheer self-indulgence. This is just a quick

message as I want to go off and play in the sea. Oops...
how's the flu?

Nobody had warned me that an aspect of travelling on your own
is that you sort of morph into another being, which just adds to
the unexpected fun of the adventure.
Weather-wise, one thing of note is the abundance of 'liquid
sunshine', which here refers to the rain and not the amber
nectar of Oz. This is not really a problem as it cools everything
down for a fraction of a second but the relief is only temporary
as the rain also ensures that the humidity is high. Head in the
proverbial clouds and back on the road, my search for a t-shirt
met with success so, as a reward, it was time to change the pace
and seek out a little culture with a visit to the museum. By the
time I found it, tucked away, the doors were closing for lunch. So
I mooched around various roads and tracks and photographed
the flora and fauna of the island and visited the old whitewashed
coral built church (1853). It's hard to imagine living somewhere
where everything except fish, coconut, coconut derivatives,
fresh fruit and vegetables has to be imported from New Zealand.
(On reflection, I suppose the UK isn't exactly a world leader in
the self-sufficiency stakes). The Cook Islands used to export
bananas and copra and enjoy a degree of financial independence
through its trading. However, today the island nation is too
small to compete commercially and is now heavily reliant on
the tourist trade for income. Kerchink! I was more than happy
to add something to the islands' coffers.

Once again, it was time for a little something, so I refreshed
myself with a fresh orange juice at Blue Note Café, where 'Pa'
of the famed volcano/cross island walks is based. His striking
dreadlocks made him unmissable, and I'm not sure why I didn't
ask him to escort me on an energetic trip up and over 'them,
there hills' – the sharp cone of Te Rua Manga (The Needle) and
the flat topped Raemara. Possibly the thought of expiring at the

top from heat exhaustion, was a deterrent. Instead, dawdled back through town passing the Cooks Corner bus stop to the last hat shop where I completed my shopping mission. My crowning glory was chosen in desperation (it's hot ambling around in the midday sun) rather than for any sartorial edge it gave me over my fellow travellers.

Continuing my island circumnavigation, I caught the two o'clock clockwise bus and sat back to enjoy a somnambulistic journey, peeking heavy-lidded over hibiscus-festooned hedges watching the leisurely pace of Rarotongan life. In the heady warmth of the afternoon, the sights, sounds and smells envelop you in a cosy sensory-blanket and gradually the effort of keeping your eyes open begins to feel like an unnecessary waste of energy. Only the fear of sleepily drooling from flower-fuelled intoxication kept me semi-conscious with my mouth securely shut. Allowing for frequent stops a complete circuit of the island takes between forty-five minutes to an hour. The bus travels in both the clockwise or anticlockwise directions, and a return fare can bought for the princely sum of four dollars.

Back at the hotel, I walked along the road to a local store to seek out necessary supplies; water, beer and peanuts. The peanuts provided me with an adequate salty lunch, the water sipped as a constant top-up and the beer would be consumed later, sitting on my balcony. By mid-afternoon, it was time to test the snorkel again. This time I ventured further away from the hotel to the far side of a sand-spit and in this new location had even better luck with the sea-life. At this stage I still wasn't really sure what I was looking at or what was looking at me. I was fascinated by a sleek silver arrow, about two feet long from tip to tail with two thirds of its body taken up by its pointy snout, which hung in the water motionless gazing at me with two kindly, but inquisitive eyes (am I romanticising about a *fish*?) I'd like to think it thought the same of my orbs, blinking back at him from behind my mask, but I doubt I was creating such a favourable impression – and my floating bulk was no match for his silver bullet physique which, with barely a quiver, shot off his curiosity obviously sated. Inert Quink Ink blue starfish and knobbly sea slugs occupied the sands, whilst anemones and sea urchins staked out their territory on the corals, and above and around whizzed gar fish, wrasses, angel fish and parrot fish – and me. Oh what bliss!

Three hours later, looking rather the worse for wear, I headed for the bar where, forgetting my earlier purchase, I knocked back a glass of draught beer – almost in one. Whether it was my sea swept appearance or the dribbly way I guzzled the much-needed liquid refreshment, either way I obviously less than impressed the barmaid who seemed reluctant to return my *I'm in heaven – I'd spring a cartwheel if I could* beery smile.

My floating bulk was no match for his silver bullet physique…

During my temporary single status, there were very few occasions when I felt any discomfort at being a singleton and when I did, it was usually because I was in the middle of nowhere without another soul in sight. Oddly, because this was a peopled-paradise, the first twinge was at the Beach Resort. Perhaps less than a week into my adventure my antennae were being hypersensitive, or perhaps some Cook Islanders are less cheery than others, especially in the presence of a middle-aged lady who's rather enjoying herself... and the beer. I'm quite certain that my sea/salt/sand appearance was rather more mumsy than sexy, but for whatever reason, the barmaid continued to scowl.

Happily by the end of my stay, there was only one (similarly middle-aged) waitress left who wasn't either chatting to me or at least returning my smile in a polite way. It was the barmaid who had disdainfully served me with that first pint. She determinedly refused to return my ever broadening smiles, and I sensed that if she could she would have handed me my beer via long tongs. Disapproval radiated from her every pore, delighting me. Not being renowned for my rebellious exploits, here was someone 'tut-tutting' over my nightly beer-swilling activities (two pints on a good night). Hooray for frowns, I felt liberated! Although, on reflection, from what I'm not really sure.

Back at home, lazing in the bath is a daily form of bliss, but after hours submerged in seawater, nothing beats standing under a cool shower. The powerful hotel shower plus the delicious island coconut soap equalled an ideal restorative at the end of a busy day in paradise. Refreshed, thumbing through the hotel information, I read that Monday night was curry night, with a flamethrower providing the entertainment. Uncertain if this was a coded warning that the curry was going to be HOT, or just the hotel supporting local talent, either way it seemed a reasonable ending to the day. Selecting something cool to wear, I studied my shoe options: the trainers which had played a lead role in my departure from London, coral creepers which kept a safe distance between my toes and the spiky things on the sea bed or a pair of patent leather strappy evening shoes. No contest really. Clad in black patent I clattered down the steps from my room, scrunched over Muscle Beach reminiscent sand encrusted pathways and squeaked towards my destination. Unsurprisingly, the next night I chose the fourth option and, with eyes down, sallied forth shoeless as all things many-legged scuttled into and out of my path.

Returning to curry night and its promised entertainment. As I neared the restaurant the now familiar sounds of melodic Polynesian voices greeted me. Two chaps, accompanying themselves on guitar and ukulele, sang with gusto and passion to, I imagined, an entranced audience. As I rounded the corner my dismay must have matched theirs as, in a sea of empty seats, my lonely table for one was going to make a considerable difference to the attendance figures. Where was everyone? How could they sing so passionately to so few? And where was the flamethrower?

With a sad inevitability, guest numbers had fallen since the September 11th atrocities but as Easter approached they were creeping up again. Most visitors to the Cook Islands are from Australia, New Zealand, the UK and Germany – with virtually no tourists from Asia. Although guest numbers were down, the hotel's kitchen seemed oblivious. Having dithered about where to sit (too much choice), I watched as the waitress, with a shake of her head, removed unwanted cutlery and glasses from my table; she thought it very sad that I was eating alone. Curry night being buffet night, I made my way towards a blue haze of meths hovering over acres of chaffing dishes, where I further dithered about what to eat (again, too much choice). Not wishing to inflict the same sense of disappointment on the kitchen staff that the singing duo must have been enduring, I dutifully worked my way through a mouth-watering selection of curries and sambals.

Returning from a second gluttonous foray amongst the chaffing dishes, I realised that I had been sitting with my back turned to the only other occupied table at which sat the friendly couple from Derbyshire and so spun round for a quick chat. We were becoming quite familiar, as we'd also met at the internet shop in Avarua where they were buying a telephone card as they were still failing to make contact with home via the hotel and wanted to try the local phones. Anyway, by Monday night they were swinging between a laidback "it's OK" approach to one of sheer panic as they wondered what was happening at home, imagining of course the very worst of scenarios. Failing to reach assorted grandparents the sheer panic mood swings were beginning to far outnumber the ever more timid "I'm sure it's fine really" attempts to soothe one another.

As I left my table for another early night, I wished them good luck with the telephones and said that I wouldn't be shadowing them on the morrow as I was heading for Aitutaki Island and the day after they were off to New Zealand. Although NZ is a fairly large country, I sort of imagined that I would bump into them in some remote spot, still clutching a phone card and looking ever more distressed. Back in my room, I spent half an hour deciding what might be needed for tomorrow's adventure and lined up the chosen items, ignorant of the fact that a passport might have been handy. Had I not read the guidebook cover to cover? Satisfied with my choices, I climbed into bed and once again as my head hit the pillow... curtains. *Why isn't it like this at home?*

Tuesday 26th March: another flight and serious sunburn

I beat the 6am alarm call by fifteen minutes, giving myself time for a leisurely cup of tea accompanied by a few pages of *The Skull Mantra* an excellent holiday read – an intriguing murder/mystery with a bit of Buddhist enlightenment thrown in for good measure. A happy bon voyage gift from my sister, Josephine, and a greater temptation than my unopened Open University books which were taking up ten of my fifteen kilo baggage weight: Brecht on the beach... I don't think so. An hour later I was wandering around the hotel garden waiting for my transport, which finally arrived on a whim rather than to collect a named individual. I'm still not sure how or why the driver turned up as neither I nor the hotel appeared on his list but he'd decided to call in at the Beach Resort anyway.

Rarotonga's Domestic Departures Terminal is basic, just some weather proofing to cover the two check-in desks from the worst of any rain, but totally adequate. I thought the tray sitting on one of the check-in desks covered with a tea towel might have been the in-flight catering... and it was: fresh muffins. I chatted to Tammie from Alberta who was rather dubious about the airworthiness of the Saab 340 (a twin turbo prop thirty-four seater). Digging into my fund of aircraft knowledge, I reassured her by saying that small planes were particularly nifty at scrambling up through clouds, embellishing this fact with the further fact that they are used for flying into the eye of storms. Inevitably my enthusiastic words made her glance nervously skywards, where indeed a hefty blanket of clouds was obscuring the volcanic peaks. Judging by her worried scowl, I don't think I had given her the reassurance she was seeking.

Clouds were not the only concern. The tiny plane would probably have made my husband's brow furrow a little, had he been standing on the tarmac at eye-level with the tiny cockpit. Through a hole just below the cockpit's windscreen, the pilot's hand appeared and into it the dispatcher placed a copy of the flight manifest, or possibly a shopping list or maybe both. The disembodied hand withdrew silently into the aircraft leaving the hole seemingly open to the elements and air pressure; perhaps we were only going to skim the wave tops. The configuration was one seat, the aisle and two seats, with a row of four seats at the back. From 3A I had an unobstructed view of Helena, the immaculate flight attendant, as she worked in a galley no wider than her shoulders which simultaneously brushed both sides of the tapered space. She was efficient, speedy and charming and in forty minutes had fed and watered passengers and flight crew and diligently washed and cleaned the equipment she had used.

The arrival at Aitutaki was even more chaotic than the arrival at Rarotonga had been, but as ever the mayhem began to subside and miraculously everyone found themselves on the right tour with the right guide. Ours emerged from the cockpit where he'd squeezed in behind the pilot and greeted us with a row of dazzling white teeth which complemented his cheery demeanour. The fact that I was travelling without any sort of papers or tickets just wasn't an issue. Try commuting in London with just a "good morning" as your ticket.

The first part of the day was a trip round half of the volcanic island. It's much smaller than Rarotonga with just one pointy cone. The largest volcano on Rarotonga, Raemara, has a flat top and according to legend, the pointy bit flew off and landed on Aitutaki. Sad but inevitable the population which currently nudges 2,000 is dwindling. The island pays for students to receive degree level education in (typically) Fiji or New Zealand but graduates must then return to the island to give back three years of work. Those parents who can afford it pay for their children's education, so that they can enjoy better career prospects as soon as they have graduated by circumnavigating the three year requirement. Four of the Cook Islands' presidents since independence in 1960 have come from Aitutaki and the islanders are rightly proud of their political nous.

The first stop was a visit to the main town, just a couple of shops and at least twice as many churches. The island's predominant religions are the Cook Islands Christian Church, 7th Day Adventist, Church of the Latter Day Saints, plus a further smattering of Presbyterian non-conformist churches and one Catholic Church. Christianity arrived via the London Missionary Society and, with apologies, some of the items in the shops looked as if they had been brought to the island by the original Christian missionaries. I have never seen such rusty tins of food for sale, and I'm not talking a little discolouration, I mean rusted through to the point where the contents were just a rust atom away from explosive freedom. With the best will in the world, a display of rusty tins can never look truly enticing to the avid shopper. *Perhaps they'd be more appealing as an art installation?*

A drink came next then a stroll by the quayside before returning to our transport for the remainder of the journey. We bounced along in an open truck of mixed origins with wobbly bench seats and a wooden canopy providing intermittent shade until we reached the Pearl Beach Resort where our boat was moored. It too seemed of hybrid parentage and was necessarily large as it was already teeming with islanders and tourists. The Rarotongan arrivals found seats where they could, stumbling and lurching as the boat waddled from its moorings (it wasn't a pretty boat) and then headed across the shimmering water to the tiny blot of an island. This island's claim to fame was that it played host to the TV *Survivors* programme: who could survive on a desert island the longest, complete impossible tasks and not get stabbed in the back by a fellow castaway. It was tiny, had been a leper colony and was now home to wild pigs and chickens. It took about three and a half minutes to walk around. The highlight of this stop on our itinerary was a demonstration of 101 things to do with a coconut. And I got to drink some fairly grubby coconut cream and smear it on my arms as sun oil: *m'm, m'mm.* Before the demo we'd been allowed a quick swim which served to whet the appetite for what followed.

Back on the boat and off to enjoy a snorkelling session. Aitutaki and its sister islands are part of an atoll circling an enormous lagoon. So wide is the lagoon that when crossing it you get a 360 degree view of water and sky separated by a frilly white collar of surf. From the middle of the lagoon, the few islands look like green smears on a pure white shirt-collar and up above, like an upturned pudding basin, stretches a canopy of the deepest sky blue. The colour of the water is the brightest and clearest turquoise and sparkles like a liquid gem. The sand which fringes the islands and carpets the lagoon is a dazzling white. Happy to be back in water, but having been spoilt by the abundance of fish at the bottom of my temporary garden, I simply floated whilst squinting up at the glorious sunny sky – a treat beyond measure. Whichever way around we chose to wallow, a fun time was had by all.

A blast from a conch shell summoned the end of playtime and a return to the mother ship where lunch was served as we cruised towards One Foot Island. The highlights of lunch were barbequed fish, a bit like tuna, coleslaw, lots of exotic fruit and a yummy coconut pudding. Tammie, having lived about as far from the sea as you can possibly get had never eaten fish, and didn't seem keen to experiment. After much coaxing from our tour guide and yours truly, she managed a few mouthfuls but judging from more of her facial expressions, didn't appear to share my view that this was a meal worth waiting for. I had hoped she might be warming to my motherly coaxing.

A long spit of sand edged by shallow water led to our island destination and several of us opted to slip from the boat to wade across the first watery grains of sand towards the shore. We paddled, chatted and watched a magazine photo-shoot, which had been going on for ages signifying the models' stamina. I'm surprised they didn't simply keel over in the glare of the sun. And just how many shots are needed to get the right one? Surely there is only so much you can do with sun, sea, sand and a skinny girl in a scanty bikini?

Nearing dry land, the thought was beginning to dawn that perhaps walking over white sands in ferocious sun had been less than sensible. Consequently, a posse of lobster-like tourists waded ashore in front of the Post Office, the only building on the island. The beach bar doubles as a post office where passports can be stamped – a great bit of tourism savvy. So, now I realised why passports might be needed as a surprising number of people, including Tammie, produced their passports from the folds of their beachwear for a One Foot Island stamp. We all bought postcards and sent them home, writing with a wobbly collection of biros, which had been squirreled away by the 'post master'.

A wander around the island, a drink and then back into the water and it was fabulous – this time the marine life had decided to come out and play. But I was beginning to feel the heat and found swimming in a water-logged t-shirt heavy going. Anyway, mustn't grumble as the whole day was magnificently memorable, a view shared by my fellow travellers – even the very seasoned ones who had been here, there and everywhere seeing and doing everything. One of whom obviously thought that travelling solo with a suitcase, even one called George, was nothing like travelling solo with a backpack, especially if the environment meant that it had to be slung over your stomach for safety's sake. I obviously have a lot to learn, so naturally kept very quiet about my very non-backpackers hotel room: no shared lavatorial facilities for me. Nor did I mention my addiction to an evening squirt of Dior perfume, even if it was appropriately called *Dune*.

After two hours it was back on board the boat for a gentle drift back to Aitutaki. The resort itself is just as wondrous as it should be in such surroundings. I sat on a sun deck overlooking the beach glugging a refreshing lemonade and bitters and thinking 'this is the life'. Half an hour later it was back to the bus and judging by the general foot-shuffling, the effect of a day in the blistering sun was beginning to take its toll as a now bedraggled party meandered its way over a small bridge heading for the bus. Glancing down, you could see clusters of the most enormous clams – and I do mean enormous. Judging by the corals growing on them they must have been ancient. Equally ancient, our transport stood ready. This time it was a brightly painted wooden frame perched over, we were soon to discover, a spring-free chassis, which hit each and every bump in the road with a spine-shaking *thwack*.

With the backs of my legs beginning to feel a tad painful I climbed onto the bus where, as one, we began to inspect bits of our bodies that were suffering from sun burn. Having liberally doused myself in increased factor – factor 25 I had forgotten the backs of my legs and as a result they had fried to the point of *bien cuit* by rays of the sun bouncing off and being magnified by the gleaming white crystalline sand. *Ouch, ouch, ouch.* The drive back to the airport completed the circuit of Aitutaki. Arriving at our destination it was soon apparent that all formalities had long since been dispensed with; no sign of check-in or customs just friendly chaos and a chap playing the electric organ and belting out Country and Western songs with the occasional Polynesian contribution. I'm not sure that we were capable of stretching our faces to bestow smiles of appreciation. But I guess he'd seen sunburn before.

After some lengthy milling about our flight finally arrived from Rarotonga and inbound and outbound passengers were swept up in the now anticipated mêlée which, like the Red Sea, parted suddenly, as each group set off in the appropriate direction. Back on board, wondering what damage the belated globs of sun lotion on the backs of my legs would do to the leather upholstery, we were greeted by Ingrid. An extremely welcome beer and nibbles appeared only to disappear in rude haste and in no time we were bouncing back to earth on Rarotonga.

How remiss! I have forgotten to describe our guide for the day, (another) George. Built like a rugby prop forward, or whatever, with slim ankles holding up bulging calves topped by enormous solid (I imagine) thighs and shoulders that Atlas would have envied: a solid inverted triangle. George was a mine of information, always jolly, a dab hand with a coconut and blessed with the most amazing singing voice. Accompanying himself on the ukulele he flashed teeth as white as the Aitutaki sand as he pledged his love to Tammie, who I think was rather smitten. Wonder if they kept in touch? When he climbed into the cockpit for the return flight a wag in our party quipped, "By George, he can fly too!"

At seven in the evening I arrived back at the hotel and went straight to my room where, as if attacked by a cattle prod, I jumped into and out of and danced around the shower, trying to keep the water away from the backs of my legs. A tub of Aloe Vera provided a soothing respite and barefoot I plodded back to the restaurant area and bought a toasted focaccia filled with camembert, ham and cranberry – is this the Cook Islands? – and slithered my way back to my room to munch in solitude. By nine o'clock I could keep my eyes open no longer and headed for bed, expecting sleep to elude me, but as it was suddenly four in the morning that obviously hadn't been the case. The heat radiating up from the sheets could have reheated the leftover portion of my focaccia so I cooled things down with a further liberal dose of assorted creams and lotions, trying to massage some life back into my very red skin which had become so taut I was beginning to dread what the next stage of my sunburn might bring: it would be no chrysalis to butterfly moment.

Consequently, as others feed one-armed bandits, so I fed the slot on the hotel's 'mini mart' vending machine… feeling as if I had struck 'three cherries' when yet another tube of after-sun thudded into sight. Back in my room, I further depressed myself by realising that my new camera had a sun, sea and sand setting which might have been rather useful in the sun, sea and sand setting of Aitutaki.

Wednesday 27th March: hello to Mr Picasso

Unsurprisingly, I enjoyed a quiet day with the morning taken up by writing my journal whilst sitting in the shade. Lunch was a refreshing Greek salad, eaten whilst perched on the very edge of my chair. In the afternoon I pottered back to my room for more libations of Aloe Vera and a snooze. At three I awoke fearful that a day on this glorious island was passing by without any participation on my part, so mask and snorkel at the ready, I headed off to the beach and settled on a spot still further away from the hotel, where the water looked a little deeper.

Picasso Trigger Fish... small, territorial and not afraid to nip...

Face down in my watery wonderland, all smarting thoughts of ninth degree burns disappeared and I found myself face to face with a small, colourful fish who peered at me through round bright eyes perched, seemingly, half way down his back (I had never registered the position of fish eyes before). Stripes, splashes and spots of just about every colour under a tropical sky made him look particularly beguiling. I looked at him, he looked at me. But this wasn't the gentle eye of the Wrasse eyeing the intruder. The fish darted from view and then reappeared on my right side, he then darted towards my feet and began – this sounds so silly, he was tiny, the size of a small sardine – chasing me, and all I could think was, 'He can't be serious.' But he was. I took a few minutes to react, watching his antics enthralled, but I finally got the message: I wasn't welcome. So this was the dramatically coloured, aptly named Picasso Trigger Fish, small, territorial and not afraid to nip. He won and I moved off to explore elsewhere.

At sunset I headed back to my room, showered, squeezed the last drop of Aloe Vera from the tube and indulged in a supper of Fosters and peanuts before settling down to the travellers' task of postcard writing, with just the rustle of lush green leaves swaying gently outside my bedroom window for company. Not a bad environment in which to write 'wish you were here...' messages home.

Whilst on the subject of home, emailing to those still hoping for the warm arrival of an English spring, I thoughtlessly enthused:

Next came the crystal clear waters and sparkly sands of the Cook Islands. The excellent snorkelling was a welcome relief from the heat and humidity but I should have thought to buy a disposable underwater camera as no one will believe my descriptions... the clams really were HUGE. Against a background of grey coral, the multicoloured fish gave the coral surface a Jackson Pollock paint-spattered appearance. I would also have liked to photograph the Picasso Trigger fish as he so small and me so large, but still he managed to scare me away from his territory – full marks for his bravery and zero for mine.

Thursday 28th March: sob, sob – a last day in Paradise

Not much to report today. Spent the morning photographing my surroundings and remembering to use 'night setting' for the beach scenes (think that helps counteract the glare – we shall see). Went into town to check emails and search out the museum, where sadly it took all of thirty seconds to view the Cook Island Maori artefacts as all the good examples have been spirited away to the British Museum. However, what I did find was a faded poster which named all the fish I had seen and quite a few I hadn't. With piscatorial names floating in my head, drifted back to the hotel on the one-twenty bus and caught up with more informed journal writing. *Phew*, now up to date, but for how long?

As a reward, I went off to play again with the marine life. *Oh, how I will miss this.* Which reminds me, must be careful as there are strong currents. At first I hadn't been aware of them, but on Wednesday afternoon they were running very strongly. So, for exercise, I swam up against the current and then hung in the water like a large piece of blubber and let the current carry me back down towards the hotel, which it did very rapidly. Was thoroughly enjoying the ride until about the fourth go when the current swept me close to some coral which was home to sea urchins with very long spines and, basically, I panicked! I didn't fancy picking spines out of my burnt legs, so that brought the day's fun and games to a halt. Although the currents were running gently today, the water had become murky due to the churning motion of yesterday's tides. As a result, I kept coming up against 'things' unbeknown to me and after a time I began to pine for an aquatic chum to go *oooh* or *eeek* with, but I wasn't really complaining about my lone water activities. And should I admit this? When head down in the water, I do hum to myself. Not sure why, but it's just automatic. The fish don't seem to notice.

Eventually, as the light faded and the evening calm began to settle over the water, I retreated from the beach for one last time. I walked towards the hotel with mixed feelings: I had so enjoyed my magical visit to the Cook Islands but tomorrow's dawn would bring the start of a new adventure as I was heading to North Island, New Zealand. Back in my beautiful room, I packed my bits and bobs, squirreling away a bar of the soft soap, and 'dressed' for a dinner of bland tuna, that was only so-so when compared to the delicately spiced curry.

On my final night sleep did evade me, so I got up at four and breathed my last gasps of heady tropical air before preparing for the next leg of my travels. The earlier twinges of solo uncertainty had vanished and after the luxury of relaxing in the sun and the sea, I was now eager to tackle the energetic challenges of extreme New Zealand.

North Island, New Zealand

Friday 29th March: dry those tears and welcome to Extreme New Zealand

A very short day! Left the hotel as dawn was breaking and chatted to a couple from Richmond, Yorkshire. He had taken early retirement from British Airways two years ago and was delighted that he had, because now they were travelling as real fare-paying passengers – staff standby having long since lost its appeal. As, likewise, an ex BA employee (of several decades ago) I couldn't resist taking a quick scoot down memory lane, but they didn't reciprocate my gabbled enthusiasm for the days of 'trying a little VC-tenderness', with 'the world's favourite airline'. Perhaps it was the hour of the day.

Unfortunately, they seemed equally unimpressed about their stay on Rarotonga as neither snorkelling nor sun-bathing were their thing. What, I wondered, had they imagined they might do on a tiny tropical island? However, they were one up on me as they had discovered the botanical gardens which proved to be the highlight of their stay. I missed the gardens which was a great pity as they were probably awash with exotic splashes of tropical colour. But you should always leave something unseen and then you have a reason to return.

Perhaps next time I ought to bring my now convalescing husband with me...

Hot cross buns for breakfast on the flight reminded me that it was Good Friday. Just four hours fifteen minutes after our early morning departure we were suddenly circling above a sea teeming with tiny boats before coming in to land at Auckland – on Easter Saturday. The International Date Line seems a bizarre concept.

Saturday 30th March: a drive north to Whangarei, Bay of Islands region

Auckland looked stunning from the air. Built on seventy-one (how did they count?) volcanic cones it is one of the few cities in the world to have two harbours on separate major bodies of water: the Pacific Ocean and the Tasman Sea across which white sails fluttered in all sea-going directions. Anxious to explore, I swiftly collected my upgraded red Mitsubishi Lancer (thank you very much), hefted George into the cavernous black void of the boot and was away – heading north accompanied by the rhythmic thuds of my case sliding about in its unfettered domain. I quickly decided that at road level Auckland looked too large and sprawly to be tackled in the time I had available, so next visit (there would surely be one) I would plan to spend at least two days in the city before picking up a car.

The journey north was more tiring than I thought. The maximum speed limit is 100kph, but everyone hangs annoyingly on your tail as obviously no one but a tourist drives at 100kph. The frequency of curves, dips and bends kept me alert and my suitcase busy. And all around the weird primordial vegetation offered a stark contrast to the tumbling profusion of colourful flowers that I had left behind on the Cook Islands. This was every shade of green, with wild Pampas grass swaying in great clusters and palms which looked like ferns growing out of telegraph poles, commonly known as tree ferns (that's the sort of imaginatively descriptive name I could come up with).

Not many towns on my route and those I did whiz through were... dead; Easter holidays and no one at home. Met a few showers, nothing much, and the temperature was comfortably warm. Sadly, I passed very few stopping places and the large loose stones on the supposedly 'hard' shoulder were uninviting, so found it difficult to pull over. When I did, my camera failed to record the scale of the scenery. How unfortunate because the countryside I was driving through was breathtaking in its beauty, but obviously the road planners didn't think that drivers might like to stop and admire it, so there were no strategically placed scenic photo spots.

So what was I looking at? It always seems wrong to compare somewhere to a place that's known, but to say it reminded me a little of Devon might give a hint of what the view was like. But if Devon is squished up – this is spread out with bigger horizons. Then again, if I think about the geology of this section of North Island, surely the hills are too jagged signifying their volcanic heritage to be likened to the rounded, well-worn Devonian landscape? Yet it's not quite the pushed up mountains of the Tyrol (there are a lot of Germans here – I think living, rather than tourists). Point proved – it is wrong to compare places. Instead, I shall just enjoy the unique scenery of New Zealand as it unfolds before my steadily advancing Lancer.

Stopped at a tiny coffee shop in the middle of nowhere for a drink and a sarnie and unwittingly sampled my first portion of southern hemisphere beetroot: it crops up in all sorts of dishes as a, none too subtle, purple garnish. Happily I like beetroot. Sated, I then pushed on to Whangarei, where I did a few circuits of the town before finally finding the Quality Hotel. Checked in at about two-thirty in the afternoon and then spent the rest of the day absolutely whacked: in 'extreme New Zealand' should I be concerned about this apparent lack of stamina? Not too tired to launder some clothes and then potter, potter, potter. Roast pork for supper, with that ubiquitous garnish, provided a short-lived energy boost before tiredness swooped in and it was shutters down. Further note to self: am I recording too much eating? I do seem to do be doing a lot of it. Plus the beer consumption is continuing at a steady pace.

On leaving my palatial quarters in Rarotonga, I knew that it might be some time before I again experienced such opulence. Although I was hardly staying somewhere which required me to carry my worldly goods strapped across my stomach, the drab brown room which George and I now occupied did not live up to my expectations of quality in a hotel named Quality. Certainly adequate though. And a bit more back-packer like.

Sunday 31st March: putting the Lancer through its paces

Up early and on the road just after nine, although it did require a few more circuits of Whangarei before I finally found the road north. Hopes to fulfil a full day's pre-planned agenda were soon dashed when I realised that distances and travel conditions were conspiring against me. Headed first for Russell, via the Opua ferry, and arrived at this delightful white-washed town once renowned for its seedy reputation. It started life as a pioneer settlement and whaling station, swiftly gaining a reputation for lawlessness, thereby earning the sobriquet of the 'hell-hole of the Pacific', a label hard to imagine as the neat buildings twinkled innocently in the sunshine. Apparently all twenty-four brothels, in a town no bigger than – well, somewhere quite small – were kept busy by a testosterone fuelled clientele of deserting seamen, runaway convicts, grog sellers, as well as the less itinerant settlers and traders.

The bewitchingly eclectic Russell Museum was crammed

with all sorts of memorabilia from the pioneering days, plus whaling, fishing and sailing bits and bobs and a one fifth scale model of Cook's *Endeavour*. Really, anything and everything that represented life in Russell one hundred and fifty to two hundred years ago, was on display, including the many *Rules for Teachers*, circa 1915 (Kate, are you paying attention?): 'You may, under no circumstances, dye your hair... You may not loiter downtown in ice cream parlours... You must wear at least two petticoats...' Perhaps the town's 'hell-hole' reputation required the board of educational trustees to be particularly cautious regarding the moral well-being of their female teachers.

Amongst the memorabilia were whalebone scrimshaw artefacts, such as a pipe rack and knife handle. Scrimshaw being any handicraft produced by sailors idling away their (I imagine) rare spare moments and for those men on the whaling boats, whalebone would have been a readily available material. I picked up an information sheet which bore the following short saucy poem – it describes what could have been a gift from one of Russell's miscreant sailor's to his sweetheart:

Accept, dear girl, this busk from me;
Carved by my humble hand.
I took it from a sperm whale's jaw,
One thousand miles from land!

In many a gale, has been the whale,
In which this bone did rest,
His time is past, his bone at last,
Must now support thy brest. [sic]

The poem was etched on a whalebone busk, the rigid element of a corset placed at the centre front, and I have since discovered that is cited in Clifford W Ashley's book entitled *The Yankee Whaler*.[1]

After the culture with its emphasis on the bawdy and profane, I wanted to visit the sacred in the shape of the church, Christ Church, which is the oldest in New Zealand: a pretty, tiny whitewashed building. But it was Easter Sunday and a service was in full swing, so instead I pottered amongst the headstones, noting that several marked the premature demise of whalers, until it started to rain.

The deluge ensured that I did what I always do at times like this – had a cup of (excellent) coffee. A fellow coffee drinker handed me her Sunday newspapers and I suddenly felt very cosy and comfortable. Eventually, the road beckoned and I ambled back to the car, feeling just a little sad to be leaving such an atmospheric and welcoming spot. The ghosts of those hard bygone days do not roam the streets with any form of menace or malice.

Back on the ferry again and on to Paihia, which has an aquarium I wanted to see. By the time I arrived it was getting late, so I decided to give the fish a miss (after all, I had been swimming with their liberty-loving cousins) and head for the main item of the day – Waitangi, where the Treaty of 1840 was signed whereby the indigenous Maori population handed over their beloved country to Britain. I really enjoyed my visit as it was yet another stunningly beautiful spot, although the history did make one particular British individual feel a little uncomfortable.

To one side of the splendid colonial Treaty House, sits the Whare Runanga or Maori Meeting House a potent symbol of tribal prestige and a monument to the tribal ancestors. The building is given life with the 'Koruru' at the apex of the roof representing the ancestor's head, the ridgepole his backbone, the bargeboards his arms and inside the rafters represent the ribs and chest of the ancestor. The meeting house contains carvings from each Maori tribal area and alongside the building sits a magnificent Maori war canoe; the world's largest and built from three giant kauri trees. It was not quite a whistle-stop visit, but once again I felt a reluctance to move on as the environment was so calmly tranquil.

The next attraction on my agenda was a little further north at Kerikeri, where stood an 1821 mission house, New Zealand's oldest standing European wooden building and inhabited until 1974. Nearby the stone store is the oldest stone building in the country. Again, a perfect trip in peaceful pastoral surroundings to see buildings and artefacts all beautifully and lovingly restored and preserved by the New Zealand equivalent of the National Trust... and if I had had my membership card about my person, I could have visited the site for free, as they operate a reciprocal arrangement. I've learnt the hard way that you can never do too much preliminary research, although I could hardly begrudge my entrance fees.

Oh dear, another site was suddenly scratched from my itinerary. I had intended visiting the hot spring at Kaikohe, but the lateness of the hour, the creeping cold and the now incessant rain sent me in the direction of a 'quality' hot bath... and a plate of roast beef. I slept like a log until five in the morning when the bloke in the next room started snoring basso profondo. Anyway, can't complain as Sunday had been tippety tops. Fabulous coastal scenery, marred only by a slight panic when I decided that I ought to eat something and stopped in a winery area for a fairly yucky piece of quiche garnished with, well I needn't tell you, bleeding colourfully into the partially cooked eggy concoction. Whilst the food was enough to cause panic, in fact it was the realisation that I had lost my car keys which really quickened my heart rate. Scrabbling in vain through my bag, pockets, etc., I finally retraced my steps back to the loo where they sat waiting patiently perched on top of the hand dryer. Hey ho, there are probably worse places to be stranded!

Monday 1st April: a drive to the maritime museum at Dargaville and then south to Hamilton

A new month compounds the feeling that I've been away from home for weeks whilst in fact this is day eleven of my absenteeism. This journey was never intended to be about 'finding myself' but it is proving that my skill at 'finding my location' is not quite as useless as some at home had led me to believe; I don't count my orientation circuits as anything other than fact-finding. Today I was on the road before nine-thirty, this time with only a slight blip regarding my inboard navigation as I managed just one wrong turning on my way out of Whangarei. No great drama there and anyway, you see more when you take a few extra turnings.

Back on track, I headed over to the west coast to visit a maritime museum at Dargaville. I had forgotten all about the ill-fated Greenpeace protest ship *Rainbow Warrior* and there on the lawn lay its mast, the ship having been blown up in nearby Kaipara harbour. The 'maritime' aspect of the museum was a bit of a misnomer and whilst there was much pertaining to the sea, there were masses and masses of artefacts recording the lives of the early pioneers, especially those who had dug kauri tree gum from the peat bog areas. The kauri tree is becoming increasingly rare, but had been plentiful in the northlands. These noble hardwood trees exude an amber-like gum, true amber being the fossilised gum of coniferous trees from the Baltic region. Over time, kauri trees had fallen becoming buried in and preserved by the peat bogs. Pioneers, predominantly Scottish Highland and Islander crofters seeking new lives in the wake of the Highland Clearances, had come in substantial numbers to New Zealand to dig for the gum of the swamp kauri trees. The trees they were excavating were approximately 44,000 years old.

A hard life and a frugal one, recorded amongst mesmerising old sepia photographs. On second thoughts,

I should underline the lot of pioneers by saying that it was an excruciatingly tough life with scant reward. Weather-beaten individuals, both men and women, leant against their corrugated iron shacks and stared with an hypnotic intensity into the photographer's lens. It was almost painful to turn away: I wanted to know their individual stories. And who was behind the lens? I wondered about the grit and determination of the unknown photographers... they weren't carrying point and shoot cameras, but hefting cumbersome tripods on alien terrain. I could almost hear an oozing soughing sound as feet and tripod paddled viscous mud.

From the past to the almost present. As expected, there was also a display which told the tale of the *Rainbow Warrior*... although, upon reflection, not very well. The information was a bit random and just raised lots of questions, which it was impossible to find answers to. Nevertheless, this is being a bit picky as I thoroughly enjoyed the museum visit which, irrespective of its homespun feel, was very worthwhile. And the Bay of Islands sea views were picture book perfection. Although for a few moments I didn't think that I was ever going to see the views again, as the volunteer on duty was very chatty. Her son had been living in Brixton, England and she had been worried about that – but all was well now as he had moved to Sheffield. She had tried twice to get over to see him, but 'events' had prevented her from travelling. I finally extricated myself with a cheery, "Third time lucky," and went in search of my car. Fortunately, I had not let 'events' get in the way of making my journey to see my son. Yes, although I *was* on a maternal mission, I admit that I wasn't exactly taking the most direct route.

Back in the car and heading south I passed signs to the Kauri Museum at Matakohe. Having been intrigued by all I had read and learnt at the Dargaville Museum, a detour to another museum with a further nine dollar outlay seemed a must: right decision! Fortunately, I have a handy leaflet which sells a visit to the museum as being 'an excellent choice':

> Discover the mighty KAURI TREE, its TIMBER and its GUM, and PIONEERING SETTLERS in New Zealand. Outstanding displays, real exhibits, original early photos and fascinating stories await you. This huge museum provides a stimulating insight into the kauri theme... You will be inspired and impressed by this wonderful exhibition.[2]

All that upper case emphasis was no idle claim, as indeed I was both inspired and impressed. Despite the 'roll-up, roll-up' tone of the leaflet, this purpose built museum was a bit more professional than the two I had visited earlier, and it was stuffed to its glorious wooden rafters with heaps of interesting artefacts. And the hundreds of early photographs managed to tell the life of the kauri diggers more eloquently than a 'thousand words'.

The sawmill replica helped to illustrate the way in which growing trees were felled and then, together with the bog exhumed trees, cut. The gum had all sorts of uses, including varnish and lino. This unscheduled stop was an unexpected treat for a 21st-century traveller but what a desperately hard life those 19th-century pioneers must have lived. I feel only hardy crofters could or would have coped. And having made the gruelling four-month sea journey from northern to southern hemisphere, turning around when life got even tougher was probably never an option.

Change of tempo – from the inner ruminations of my brain to the inner rumblings of my tum. It's surprisingly exhausting driving across North Island and dashing into and out of museums, so I rewarded myself with a cup of coffee and a date scone (the needle on the scales must have been soaring to new heights...) and then it was back on the road. I decided to keep driving south, bypassing Auckland and heading on down to Hamilton. I know I ought to describe the route in great detail, but more of the earlier pampas-edged switchback is the best I can come up with. Driving down to the ferry on Sunday, I narrowly avoided the squashed remains of a hedgehog on the road (masses of squashed fauna everywhere). At the time I thought it a little strange that it should be a hedgehog, but on my way back, realised that it was a squashed kiwi... not really how I had hoped to see my first one!

Anyway, continuing on to Hamilton, a few heavy showers and lots of traffic kept me company. On arriving at my destination, as ever, I then spent half an hour going round in rectangles (you can't do circles on a grid pattern) until I found a fairly modest Flag Choice motel... which could have done with a lick of paint and a few creature comforts. No hairdryer and my adapter didn't work, but it was no great panic as I'm past caring about the vanity stakes. Time for my next meal and I'm not sure why I seem to get drawn to rather bleak eating establishments, as I dined in an empty canteen-like stainless steel and Formica eatery. From the basic menu I selected and enjoyed Hoki fish, a member of the hake family, followed by fresh fruit which had been cut finely and arranged artistically on a silver platter – as if to tempt a picky eater. Of course I appreciated the trouble that someone had gone to, but my platter did seem daintily incongruous in such an industrial setting. In contrast, the bottle of invigorating local beer which accompanied my meal was certainly not out-of-place and was downed with gusto.

My journal records that 'it is now 10pm and I need my shut-eye' as I was off to Cambridge in the morning and then on to Waitomo Caves for two days of adventure. There must have been a tiny twinge of apprehension because with a dramatic flourish, or perhaps a tiny prayer, I added: 'Dear reader, I hope I may return'. I then signed off the day's entry with a note that the weather had unexpectedly turned from warm to FREEZING.

Tuesday 2nd April and let the adrenalin fun begin

Ate a solitary breakfast and in spite of the continental being free, decided to upgrade for five dollars to the egg and bacon option. Absolutely scrumptious! It might have been a fairly basic hotel, but the catering was a notch or two up on most I had so far experienced. With a long day ahead, the calorific fuel seemed sensible and might stop me from eating another muffin.

Said goodbye to Hamilton (a straggly town of no great significance... oops, except perhaps to the Hamiltonians) and headed down to Cambridge, which was as lovely as its English namesake, with a very friendly atmosphere. I pottered around and wandered across the cricket pitch which was surrounded by majestic oak trees. There are more deciduous trees here than I've seen before and they are beginning to turn shades of yellow, gold and deep plum... a result of the unexpectedly cold weather. I read in the local paper that parts of North Island have had snow, which is earlier than usual.

Feeling the chill, I bought a padded sleeveless jerkin, I'm sure there's another name for this type of garment, but my brain's on holiday, a merino wool top and a pair of shapeless, sexless, fleecy trousers. Very middle aged, very practical... and very warm! From the shop next door I bought needle and thread as the trews were rather long. After a cup of tea and a quiet moment of reflection, I decided that the needles would stay in their gleaming state and be carried back to England, where I obviously need new needles as all the sewing I've done in recent years has taken its toll on my existing sharps and darners. I tell a lie, the sharps and darners have passed generation unto generation untouched in their ornate packaging and will probably continue, in this manner, on down the female line. The trousers would just be hitched-up over my expanding girth.

A bit of map reading followed and I opted to head for a minor road and then cut across west to join the SH3 and then down south to Waitomo Caves. Fabulous road, I think probably only about 45km, 40 of which I drove on my own, but a really, really lovely drive. Green undulating vistas, tempted me to stop and take pictures, and for once scenic stopping was easy. Hitting the SH3, the traffic became heavier and slowing down through Otorohanga I saw signs to the Kiwi House. Only a slight detour and I think another worthwhile one. Kiwis live in the 'northlands' of North Island where they are now an endangered species, as their habitat is under threat from the expanding human population. Additionally, where there are people, rats are never far away and kiwi eggs provide rats with a nutritious protein rich meal. The sad outcome is that whilst the rat population increases the kiwi numbers dwindle. Obviously drivers weren't helping either.

Kiwis are nocturnal and as soon as I saw the only pair they had in captivity (the name of the establishment had raised my expectations a little high) realised that the poor squished mound I had seen earlier really was, or indeed had been, a kiwi. To make up for the paucity of kiwi, the eponymous House had a high number of caged birds for the visitor to admire. In truth, most were rescue birds which wouldn't survive if released, plus an assortment of non-indigenous vagrants – birds which had flown off course during their migratory passages. These birds are kept in caged captivity as New Zealand does not want them breeding in an alien habitat and upsetting the country's ecology. Additionally, there were reptiles alongside water birds, birds of prey and owls, which eyed me with a 360 degree air of disdain unlike my busy escort. At some point along a maze of walkways I had been joined by an inquisitive fantail – a bit like a wagtail, but where one wags, the other fans. The Maori people call them messenger birds and it's easy to understand why... you really feel they are trying to tell you something with their fanning and posturing. They are all over the place and are truly delightful.

Somewhere I also saw what surely must have been a robin – brown all over, round body, shorter tail than our robin, with an unmistakeable robin eye... bright and round and looking hopefully for a handy grub that you might have about your person. Later, I was thrilled to see a picture of a North Island robin; glad I wasn't suffering from homesickness and that it really was a robin. I don't understand how a country can have flora and fauna which is so dissimilar to ours, whilst at the same time being home to indigenous species which are so similar to ours. *Robin, please explain...*

Wandering around the grounds I discovered that the upright trees with neat ferny tops are Pukas: how appropriate! And in the small shop, where for once I ignored the refreshments, I read that the Kiwi House is a breeding centre of high repute: another tick in the box for an excellent visit. A little sadly I said good-bye to my fan the fantail and set off once again for my holy grail: Waitomo Caves.

Arrived at about 2pm and checked in to the Waitomo Caves Hotel... *could this be the template for Bates Motel?* I found myself in a grotty bedroom in an old weatherboard colonial style building; it had been a Government Rest House circa 1890 and extended over the years as its uses changed. I expected 'Norman' to shuffle forth from the bowels of the building, but a cheery girl checked me in, instead. At 40 dollars a night, I wasn't going to complain about the lack of creature comforts, including hairdryer. They seem rarer than hotel washing machines which probably illustrates the needs of the average tourist: to wash/dry activity grubby garments and not care a fig about looks. [Before I'm sued by the hotel, I have just taken a look at its

2016 website... and its refurbishment has indeed lifted it into a different class: it looks gorgeous!]

Location wise, the position was and is awe inspiring. The hotel sits in a delightfully higgledy-piggledy garden, set high on a hillside giving uninterrupted views across the surrounding peaks and gullies. Leaving thoughts of Norman behind, I walked down through a shady, hidden pathway to emerge in the centre of Waitomo, which consists of an information centre, a shop and assorted adventure companies. I wasn't sure who I was booked to do what with, so decided to sort things out.

First things first, a drink and a muffin: you can have a muffin too many but they seem to be a national delicacy, and trying to find an alternative small nibble was proving fruitless. Slurping and munching contentedly, I mused over the fun I had had weeks ago, Visa card to hand, booking my adventures over the internet. Now thoughts of 'being too old to make a fool of oneself, breaking a leg, or having a heart attack' were squashing my earlier gung-ho version of never being 'too old to have fun, push boundaries, or rediscover long lost youth'. Anyway, the Lost World adventures would soon reveal which path was the more accurate.

Refreshed, I wandered off in search of the Lost World office, which nearly lived up to its name. Entering I was greeted with "Hello Vivien"... which was a bit startling. In response to a mental alarm bell clanging, my mind flashed up a series of questions: had no other suckers signed up; perhaps no aged suckers; had the office really been waiting all these weeks just for me? Baffled, I received my instructions for two days hence and felt the first flicker of nervousness.

Unperturbed by this tiny tremble, I then set off to find the black-water rafting bods, but they too seemed as hidden as the Lost World guys. I retraced my steps up the hill, along the hidden pathway and retrieved the car to drive to the head of the valley where there are caves you can walk through to see the glow worms. A chap at the ticket office thought that the Black Water Rafting Co (BWR) was probably the outfit a couple of kilometres out of town; he was right. More instructions followed and it was arranged that I should be picked up the next morning at ten not for the rafting, as that would come later, but for the Big Red experience – quad biking.

Back to a FRR-FRREEZING room for a very brave shower and down to: "Dinner for *one*?" (Waiters always make it sound as if no one else would want to dine with you). Strange choice on my part; seafood chowder, followed chicken fettuccine – half of which went in the pig bin – washed down with a couple of glasses of the house brew, a Cabernet Sauvignon Merlot, which made a pleasant change from my usual tipple of beer and bucked me up warmth-wise.

Making the most of the small internal glow created by the alcohol, I returned to my room and got undressed from my day clothes and then dressed for bed: knickers, nightie, jumper, dressing gown, socks and if I'd have had a woolly hat, I'd have put that on too. Thus swaddled, I tucked myself up in my icy single bed and watched *Ab Fab* on a tiny TV and as there was no remote control, swore when I had to crawl out of my now slightly less cold and damp bed, to switch it off.

Somehow, sleep overcame the cold and I drifted off into happy oblivion deciding that hyperthermia is probably a relatively civilised way in which to float from this world into the next.

Wednesday 3rd April: This is the life! Muddy quads and chilly black-water

The morning did not get off to an auspicious start. Having survived the night, I sleepily turned on the shower and – kerpow! The shower head suddenly flew off in an alarming fashion, leaving me to struggle with a headless water-spewing reptile. Blinded by the unexpected storm, I somehow managed to find the bits and put the shower back together. During this frantic exercise a jet of water had escaped and sprayed the entire ceiling and the wall opposite. Water slid down every surface drenching my towel and night wardrobe. And 'ouch', my bosoms and thighs were bruised by the sheer force of the water. The bruise-inducing water had woken me up like a bolt of electricity and my morning exercise had been taken dancing around in the shower. If I thought that that would be the end of both bruising and exercise, I was a little mistaken. But first of all, clean at least, I tottered down to breakfast which once again was an almost solitary affair with nothing special to report.

By nine, I was out in the sunshine feeling like a bug emerging from its chrysalis and warming itself before finding the energy to fly away. From my crow's nest vantage point I watched the comings and goings down below and the minutes ticked away as the hour of my first adventure drew closer. At ten-ish, a little red van stopped outside the village shop and eight Japanese (I think) tourists climbed aboard. The little van then made its way up the hill, disappeared amongst the trees and a few seconds later emerged at my side. Big Red was getting nearer! Sarah, the guide, introduced herself and the party of Taiwanese (wrong) teenagers, whose parents worked in Auckland. We then enjoyed a pleasant drive up the valley to a shed in the middle of a field in the middle of nowhere, home to a collection of quad bikes.

Sarah had just resigned after seven years working as a full-time primary school teacher to be an adventure guide. She continued to work occasionally as a relief teacher in her old school to keep her qualifications valid, but her new regime allowed her the freedom to indulge in her love of the great outdoors. Sarah spoke of all the travelling she had done in her back-packing days, adding that she would probably do more, but in the meantime she wasn't regretting her career change as she loved Waitomo and it would always be home. Once again, my thoughts flickered back to my daughter, whose own love of travel could well lure her away from the primary school classroom. Time would tell.

Back to business. Next we met the chap who looked after the quad bikes and he talked us through the 'what's what' of these machines and then kitted us out in overalls, helmets and wellie boots. Tasteful! The youngsters then set off with him to enjoy a gentle trail whilst Sarah, me and one other headed for the hills. And oh boy, what fun!

Quad biking was not as easy as it looked as the bikes were unexpectedly heavy. Also, you lean out of bends and not into them, which is the natural inclination; fighting inclinations and tackling inclines added to the experience. A gentle ten minutes pottering to get used to the gears – four, brakes – assorted and then up (literally) and away. What a fabulous non-green way to see the fabulous green countryside. Horseback would probably be more ecologically sound, but I was as happy as Larry with all that heat throbbing away under my bum. To be honest, my thumb control on the accelerator was a bit lurchy, but for a first timer, I don't think I did too badly. Managed to scare myself skidding round a corner with a precipice just feet away, but I jerked my thumb into action and put on full power and yippee! *Whoosh*, round I went to the sound of cheers from in front and behind (I was sandwiched between the chap, who was an experienced rider and Sarah).

It was a great adventure – the bits of me not covered by overall and boots got scratched by gorse and mud spattered, but I didn't notice until afterwards. At one point we stopped to look at the breathtaking scenery and I gratefully sent up a silent prayer to my benefactor. If on my travels I think too much about my flu-recovered husband, I do start to wobble as I contrast the selfishness of my adventures, with the selflessness of his 'freedom pass'. But the wobble is temporary. Now, back to the mud…

On our slippery journey we met up with the youngsters.

Watching the casual ease with which they rode their bikes made me think that we were on the wrong tracks, perhaps they should have been on the tougher route? Said a quick "hi" then off went the senior class (surely that wasn't a slightly smug smirk from me?) for a bit more uphill and down dale before muddily heading back to the bike shed. Parked my bike very neatly, and *yes* definitely smugly, in its allotted space!

Sarah's father, Jim, who had led the youngsters, was delightful and wanted to know if I'd enjoyed the ride and had I scared myself? "Good," he said when I confirmed "yes" on both counts. "Wouldn't have been right if you hadn't," he replied with a grin. My email home:

> This is the life! The New Zealand highlights have to include my outdoor adventures in the Waitomo Caves region. The first adventure was above ground and as the day drew nearer began to have concerns about the ecological impact of riding a quad bike over unspoilt countryside – frightening the animals and polluting the atmosphere. Regretfully, all green thoughts went from my mind as I accessed hidden gullies and climbed steep hills to survey the most incredible scenery and wonder at pockets of undisturbed ancient forest. Many of the varieties of vegetation that grow wild are in fact imports brought into the country by intrepid settlers, so it was great to see something that truly belonged: weird nikau palms, tree ferns, New Zealand flax and toetoe grass. Also managed to scare myself more than once, but that's permissible. Not sure why, but I did have great problems with lefts and rights, ins and outs, clockwise and anticlockwise…

Back to the hotel, climbing the hill via the 'fairy grotto' as I have now named the walk through the undergrowth, for a quick de-mud before gathering up my swimming togs and heading off to my black-water rafting adventure. Got there early, so had half a scone and a drink for lunch. Whilst munching, Jim came into the BWR office cum café for his lunch. We started chatting and he was so enthusiastic about Waitomo Caves and what the area had to offer and was equally enthusiastic and encouraging about what I was doing… a solo middle-aged traveller having an adventure. He was an absolute weather beaten and gnarled old charmer! When you're on your own, it's these little conversations that mean so much. And somehow it's always the fifty plus blokes who seem to say the nicest things!

Mine was quite petite compared to some…

One-thirty came around and along with my fellow rafters, was herded towards a van where I sat opposite glamorous Daphne from Santa Monica… about which we chatted as I now felt an expert on that specific point on the globe. Arrived at the site, where we were kitted out in smelly wetsuits, jackets, sock thingies, wellie boots and helmets. Everything was cold and soggy from the previous occupants. Jane, the guide, had to zip me into my wetsuit, by virtually putting her foot on my stomach and heaving on the zip in an effort to squash my matronly bosoms into one attractive mid-chest lump. The wetsuit was big everywhere else, but the bosoms were definitely a quart into a pint pot arrangement. Having managed to corral them, breathing then became a heaving optional extra.

Smelling quite unappealing, we climbed back into the van for a short trip to our testing spot. The first task was to choose a rubber inner tube. Having sat down in one, wriggled around for a moment or two and then standing up – finding it still firmly attached to your nether regions, framing your buttocks like a halo – you knew you had made the right choice. So fetching! Unusually for me, my first choice was the right choice... and I have to say mine was quite petite compared to some of the others.

The first lesson was how to form an eel; I was in the front of the long line and we all sat down on our inner tubes and grabbed the wellies of the person behind. When forming an eel in the dark, it is useful to know whether or not there is a foot in the boot you're clutching. *Ha, ha.* Then we sat on the ground to learn how to paddle forwards, backwards (to break) and turn left and right. Having mastered that little exercise on terra firma, it was off to a muddy stream where we had to prove ourselves; failure to do so meant an abrupt end to your trip. The challenge was to jump backwards from a height of six feet with the ring around your bum... not so easy if you're a wimp about heights. Having been first in the eel, I was last to jump.

Everyone else got through the task with varying degrees of finesse and when I was the 'last man standing', I knew I couldn't make an idiot of myself. But I did. I shuffled backwards to the edge of the wooden jetty, clutching my rubber ring, and flexed my knees ready to jump back into the unseen. One, two, three... and my feet stayed firmly rooted to the spot. I tried again: nothing. Jane approached with pupils dilating and I leapt backwards before she could scream "wuss". Coughing and snorting muddy water is an experience, not a good one, but I'd made it! At this point, I should add that I was the granny of the outfit, everyone else being about thirty years my junior.

From there we trudged over rocks, into a cave and on and on: me stumbling and Daphne pointing out that Jane's frosty demeanour left little to be desired. Between stumbling (well, have you tried caving in ill-fitting, water-filled wellies?) I mumbled that a smile would mean so much. But at last the black-water lake at the back of the cave loomed in the shadows of our headlamps and as one we stopped moaning as the awesome spectacle took our collective breath away. It really was another fabulous experience.

The lamp-lit journey continued with a mixture of wading and paddling. We floated past cool damp rocks and bumped into submerged soggy things clinging to the sides. We fell down unseen potholes and jumped off waterfalls, trying to avoid whirlpools that would suck us down and eventually spit us out rudely into the daylight. We formed our rehearsed eel, to eel our way through a long tunnel inhabited by glow worms. Looking more like the grub of a mosquito than a worm (in fact, the larval stage of the fungus gnat) their phosphorescent glow attracts small hapless flying insects which have been careless enough to find their way deep into the cave system. Happy to find a 'mate' they stick to the glow worms like flies on a fly paper and are slowly eaten by the shining sirens. Lolling back on my inner tube, with someone's ankles firmly in my grip, I lie looking up at the night sky, dotted with tiny stars. I'm sure Orion's Belt is down here.

Now, I haven't mentioned the cold or the young girl from Nagoya, with whom I had chatted before we plunged down into these dark depths. Overcome with maternal tendencies, I kept an eye on her, because if I was cold – she was colder. Hands and feet don't count apparently, as Jane and her fellow guide Brad were only interested in chests and heads; if they became cold, the problem was getting serious. Whilst my chest was well-insulated, the young girl from Nagoya was somewhat lacking in that department. But a few well-timed calories boosted our dipping blood-sugar levels and stoked our inner fires. Having mastered one particularly arduous 'up and under', Jane was waiting perched on a rock to hand us, as we surfaced, chocolate fish: *m'mmm*, never has chocolate tasted so good! Thank you, Jane.

Not really all too soon, as we had been submerged underground up to our armpits in cold water for over an hour, we emerged back into the muddy stream into which we'd jumped, seemingly eons earlier. The journey had taken us past stalactites and stalagmites, we had drifted through enormous caverns and scrambled through narrow gaps (tugging our rubber rings) and climbed up slippery, half seen rocks. Nearly forgot – I spent ages looking at an eel (a real one this time) deep in the cavern. They're lovely, but it must be a lonely life down there with very few companions, just the occasional trickle of wellie-clad tourists. Also saw various fossils which resembled clams or oysters; New Zealand had been under water until it was pushed up zillions of years ago.

The sheer exhilaration of actually completing the escapade intact brought on the second adrenalin surge of the day. The Big Red and Black-Water adventures had been two totally different, but two totally fabulous experiences. I would do both again… but not in a hurry, I need to warm up first!

Back to the base camp to strip off – a task that was easier said than done when everything was frozen solid, but thank heavens my constricted bosoms, could at last be released. *Phew*. A sort of shower followed and it was better than nothing, but didn't really get rid of the yucky rotten rubber suffused with rotting vegetation smells. A mug of hot soup and a toasted bagel managed to set the world to rights. Feeling less than beautiful, I was amazed to see that Daphne had managed the entire journey in that lost world without chipping her immaculate fingernails.

Well, they were acrylic.

Back in my hotel room, I showered in a more leisurely, meaningful and accident-free way and took my book down to the bar before supper: the Lion Red local brew proved to be the ideal restorative after a bout of strenuous physical activity. Then time to strip out of and climb into assorted clothes, ready for bed because tomorrow's another action-filled day of adventure. From my email home:

The next adrenalin adventure was black-water rafting. The caves are famous for many things, including glow worms, and one way to see them is to splosh through water... clasping or sitting on an inner tube, which has to fit your posterior exactly. The test to see if you're fit to undertake this activity required jumping backwards (with ring in place) into muddy water. Lovely! My knees buckled ineffectively but one glare from Jane, our macho guide, and suddenly I could have leapt from the Eiffel Tower. Maybe an ungainly entry into the water, but style wasn't the issue. The reason for the dummy run became clear as underground we had to leap backwards off crashing waterfalls, avoiding whirlpools. I kid you not, a leap in the wrong direction would have you whisked away to be spewed out somewhere uncomfortable. Oh, the indignity!

The glow worms are fascinating, like little stars sprinkled on the walls of the caverns through which we floated or stumbled. You don't have to get wet, as you can see them by taking a dry walk through a different cave, but hey, where's the fun in that? *Ouch*, I've just remembered how cold it was and how I had to rub the hands of a young girl from Nagoya who was so cold she was purple...

Thursday 4th April: time for the big one...

Once again, up with the freezing lark and time to kill before the eleven-thirty off – off to the Lost World. Had breakfast in total and absolute solitary, so chatted to Rita the waitress, who said Easter had been very busy and good for the hotel, but bad for her as she'd worked both breakfast and dinner shifts. She'd much prefer one customer at a time! Lucky me, I had her full attention. A Waitomo native she had left to travel but here she was, back home again. On her travels she'd done a fifty metre abseil and said the sense of achievement was awesome. She described her childhood playing in the magical Waitomo area where they called the limestone shapes fairy castles, playing up and over them. It seems that everyone I speak to who lives here, really loves the place. I can understand why.

After my cheerful breakfast, with an hour or so to spare, went up the road to the Black Water Rafting outfit to send an email home, but the machine was so slow that I abandoned the truncated message. Returning to the village I resorted to pen and paper and settled down to a stint of postcard writing, sitting in the sun under a cloudless brilliant blue sky. By ten-thirty it was surprisingly hot and as if sensing that this might be my last drop of sunshine for some time, I sat in its full glare lapping up the warm rays... some people will never learn. Now, picture me as I roast and write, seemingly oblivious to my leaflet's dramatic description of the journey I was about to undertake:

The Lost World adventure is a spectacular 100 metre abseil into a magnificent, sheer chasm that can only be described as an enchanting wonderland. Ferns and mosses coat massive cliff faces, it is misty, cool, strangely still and smells fresh and alive. Surrounding you is a range of breathtaking rock formations that include stalactites, stalagmites, curious bubbles, swirls and drips. It is fairyland without the fairies. This is [...] 330 feet of sheer drop off a solid platform suspended high above a rushing river. On reaching the bottom of the descent, dry caving leads to a 30 metre ascent out on a cave ladder above a deep black chasm full of rushing water.[3] [n.b. 'black' does not do it justice...]

So, that was what I was about to do and see, and herewith, for those interested in the geology of what has been created over the millennia 100 metres underground, a brief geological description. Shawls are the aptly named shawl-like folds which occur as water trickles, from side to side, down the rock-face leaving deposits of calcite – these gradually build up to create the folds. The rimstones are the calcite rims which form around overflowing underground pools. Cave corals occur as water oozes from the cave walls, depositing calcite crystals which eventually form coral-like growths. Plus, evaporation of water dripping through the limestone ceiling creates both stalactites, the icicles hanging down and stalagmites, which rise up... and when both *might* touch they form a column.

And for the naturalists, in the darkness you're never alone. In addition to the glow worms, eels, koura (freshwater crayfish) cave wetas (related to the cricket but with extra-long antennae) the lost world is home to assorted beetles, spiders and their arachnid cousins the harvestmen. These bugs of the underworld all patrol their own preferred territory within this pristine habitat.

But all this was yet to be revealed to me. Back in the sun and an hour into my diligent postcard correspondence, when once again the now familiar summons, this time I was being herded by Greg and joined a party of three others: Fiona, Lou and anonymous. To my dismay, I soon discovered that they were all climbers and had all free-fallen from aircraft... plus they were in their twenties. I was a senior couch potato who climbed nothing higher than a step-ladder and had only free-fallen out of bed.

As we exchanged pleasantries, I remained blissfully unaware of what lay in store. In all the blurb that I had read, including newspaper cuttings, the emphasis had been on the one hundred metre abseil, the highest known commercial abseil in the world. *Ho, ho...* that was only part of the story. On the drive up into the hills, Greg explained that the lost world had been discovered by railroad surveyors in 1906. The whole area we were about to enter (a large area) is littered with caves, holes and chimneys and over the years numbers of sheep and cattle have disappeared, tumbling down into the abyss.

At our destination, more blue overalls with the now familiar white wellie boots and helmets awaited us, plus the addition of a rather (to me) complicated looking harness. A quick "this does this" and "don't do that" and then off to the chasm. A clump of trees was pointed out which we were to remember. But first, a steep climb down, using the two harness ropes 'cowstailed' onto guide ropes. The process of getting from a. to b. safely required that I repeat a simple task of clipping and unclipping myself on and off the guide rope, one harness rope at a time, as I went along. I do so hate these apparently simple tasks; everyone else manages them without fuss or bother whilst I'm head down fumbling away trying to look nonchalant.

When a knot, join or securing pin attaching the guide rope to the rock face creates an obstacle, you unclip one cowstail and move it on to the next section and then move the second one across. These clasps are attached to short ropes attached to the waist of your harness. What you don't want happening is to find that you're holding both clasps, simultaneously (please don't ask...) The harness isn't very comfortable, sort of cuts into the groin, but it needs to be snug; perhaps I misunderstood the definition of snug. The Lost World blurb describes the adventure as being 'surprisingly gentle'. *Oh, really...* you decide...

Having moved slowly along the guide rope there it was – the platform from which we would descend. And almost as suddenly as the platform had appeared, there I was suspended 100 metres above the ground, legs dangling and feeling fine and dandy. No time to think about the move from having two feet firmly on the platform to sitting with bum on a waist high perch, pitched out away from the platform, to one foot still on the platform, the other entwined around the rope down which you're going to move, to suddenly having neither feet on the platform and the awful feeling of what happens if your wellie boot drops off? Had my camera with me and was soon clicking away, at goodness knows what. We all descended together. Greg had a safety rope which he clipped to each of us… didn't think what would happen to us, should anything happen to him… which is probably just as well really.

Gliding down, the chasm opens like a deep gash in the earth with ferns and mosses growing on the sides and passed these we closely float. The air gets cooler and mistier as you descend. The natural tension of the rope (it feels as if it's bolted to the ground, but it's actually hanging free) means that the descent is very slow to start and you have to feed rope up through the locking system to get moving, otherwise you'd hang there forever. The ground seems a million miles away, well one hundred metres is quite a distance. We all chatted merrily and Fiona seemed to be ahead of us when I quipped, "Put the kettle on when you get down there." Nervous tension meant that saliva was in short supply. Surprisingly, the others had found moving off from the platform more of an ordeal than I had. It seemed a lot easier than jumping backwards into muddy water with a ring around your bottom. Typically, the brief moment of 'I can do it' was soon squashed and trampled upon by what lay ahead. But of the actual descent into that incredible 'lost world', I loved every second of the fifteen minutes that it took… although the harness did get a little uncomfortable towards the end. Having descended gently, I'm not sure I'm ready to bounce down rock faces like an SAS commando, but I'd certainly abseil again, without the slightest hesitation.

Now, when I signed up to this adventure I was well aware (well, I'm not completely daft) that if you go down one hundred metres there's a fair chance that you have to regain every one of those metres to get yourself back onto the earth's surface. Well, no one had explained how that might be achieved, and I certainly hadn't asked. To précis, what followed was a chilly climb, scramble, crawl, panic, sweat, giggle, swear, sort of experience, but I didn't stumble or fall – although I did receive the occasional rear-end shove. Lou, as nimble as a mountain goat, was superb at keeping an eye on tail-end-Charlie. But I did it, I did it, I did it! And then we got to this – *um* – cavernous cavern, where I noticed a ladder, or in fact a series of ladders lashed together and pointing straight up towards where I imagined Heaven might be. Lou and I stood rooted to the spot, mouthing, "Please, no", but as Greg marched us passed them, we let out a simultaneous sigh.

The lights on our helmets were on and shadows played on the back walls of the cavern, like colossal monsters looming over us. Lights were turned off and we were surrounded by a tangible thick inky blackness. A few twinkly glow worms looked like tiny holes in a big black canvas. Lights back on and we looked around at the amazing shapes hewn over the millennia by Mother Nature. Onwards the journey continued, and I even managed to walk across a pole suspended over a mini chasm – no mean feat in ill-fitting wellie boots. At no time during this subterranean sortie did I think of 'what if' consequences. This was, for me, a true adventure.

Intact, we reached a lovely smooth rock, our picnic spot where Greg handed out more chocolate fish which we washed down with a swig of lemonade. Posing for pictures, sharing a laugh and a joke, wondering at our subterranean surroundings – so, what next? Oh no, back to the ladders. I think the next bit will give me nightmares for the rest of my life; a thirty metre perpendicular ladder to be climbed. Of course, the only way out.

One at a time, attached to a safety rope, but even so, I felt very vulnerable and I wasn't sure that I had the sheer physical strength in my arms or stamina to undertake hauling my entire muffin-laden weight up one-hundred-feet (that sounds more dramatic than the metric version). Greg went up first and it seemed an age before he tugged the rope he'd attached to Fiona and up she went at a fair pace. I turned to Lou and her partner and apologised, "Sorry… but I'm not going to be last" Mr Lou said, "No worries," he'd take that honour. It's not that I'm scared of the dark, but it was darkly dark. By now the lights on our helmets were giving out a tiny flicker and as each helmet disappeared up the ladder the light level down below diminished even more dramatically, so the last one to leave the cavern would feel as if they were being chased by an ever rising tide of inky blackness. And even with a safety rope, if you slipped you'd be swinging out into a very black nothingness, until Greg managed to reel you in like a floundering fish.

Bravely I followed Fiona – *slowly*. I stopped twice for a breather, only a second or two, I didn't want to stop longer and broadcast to the team that I was a bit of a coward about this element of the excursion. *Phew, phew…* I didn't really enjoy the climb. With each rung, all I could say was, "Oh s**t, Oh s**t." I tried to hum a happy tune, but soon reverted to "Oh s**t", etc. The smell of rusty nails assailed my nostrils adding to my discomfort. I had visions of clinging onto rusty rungs that were prematurely corroding through the constant application of nervous sweat. There was one wobbly bit where two ladders met, which didn't make life easier, but eventually I saw the light of Greg's helmet up above and a few minutes later his calm voice said, "Hold it there," as he took a photo of me emerging through a narrow gap into... another chamber. Hooray! I'd made it!! Or so I thought, because I then realised that the daylight was in fact the dim glow from the two helmet lamps that greeted me. Another five, less perpendicular ladders awaited and happily they were a doddle by comparison.

Four hours after our descent, we finally emerged into daylight and the sense of achievement was enormous. Blinking, the spot where we now stood was close to the clump of trees that Greg had pointed out to us at the start of our journey. The trees grew directly above the smooth slab on which we had gobbled our chocolate fish picnic.

So would I do it again? It was certainly (for me) a strenuous trip and even my three experienced companions felt that they'd been challenged at some stage of the journey, but what an adventure! Perhaps I wouldn't rush to volunteer to climb one hundred feet straight up, but I'd rush at a chance to abseil down... anything. And, yes, in reality of course I'd do it again. The team I had shared my day with had been fantastic company and nothing beats a rush of adrenalin for making your heart sing. I came to New Zealand seeking adventure and would now set off on the next leg of my trip feeling totally satisfied by what I'd experienced and achieved... an adventure I wouldn't have missed for the world, not even the Lost World. From my email home:

The third and final adventure was for me – the big one (they do get bigger, but there are limits to my bravery/ stupidity). The fact that my three companions were all rock climbers and half my age should have sounded small alarm bells but as they adopted me in a kindly fashion and the guide was something of a hunk, I was relaxed about life: how innocent! I had no idea what lay in store and yes, I had read the small print. For several days purple bruises reminded me of where I had been and what I had done: undertaking an endurance test that I wasn't quite expecting. The bruises came from the harness buckles – the harness wasn't just for the abseil, but also the rock climbing that followed and the buckles dug in with all the bending and scrambling and at the time I was having too much fun to notice...

Returning to the base, I downed a quick bottle of pop, didn't purchase the photo Greg had taken of me (a weird piece of financial economy) before getting back on the road as I wanted to be in Rotorua by six in the evening. I remember little of the uneventful drive, I'm sure I was concentrating but might have been dangling from a rope, and after my usual circuit in search of signposts, I arrived at the hotel just ten minutes later than my target time. The building is a handsome 19th-century restoration, with an ornate verandah running around the first floor, which would have provided the original rooms with some respite from extremes of weather.

As George and I stood four-square before the receptionist, slight confusion followed as she thought I was talking about a dinner booking when I was saying 'room' (would I take a suitcase out to dinner?). With a large portion of guilt acting as my new companion, I was finally installed in the fabulous Johnson Room. The room was certainly intended for two: the bathroom was bigger than the bedroom at the Waitomo Caves Hotel and certainly far, far superior. Well, at three times the price – so it should have been. My back-packing credentials must be set at zero.

What I do remember of the drive from Waitomo are the surreal puffs of steam that emerge from the ground as you approach Rotorua. The golf course temporarily stopped me in my tracks. You had to look twice as it was seemingly dotted with fluffy clouds which appeared to emerge at random all over the links; it looked totally otherworldly and ethereal. Unfortunately the town has a glitzy, touristy vibe, so I resolved to be the only person ever to stay at the fabulous Princes Gate Hotel, right slap bang by the lake and gardens and see nothing of them, as I had a date the next day – 30km south at Wai-O-Tapu. To be exact, and I had to be, my appointment was for ten-fifteen with the Lady Knox geyser.

But first, why was my room so hot? I felt the radiators and they were off and it was only when I caught sight of my reflection in the bathroom mirror that I realised I was suffering from external combustion. My outdoor postcard writing session that morning had given me a bright red face; I was burning. The bath was beckoning and I couldn't wait to ease my weary limbs into a froth of warm soapy bubbles. Stripping off, again in front of the too-large mirror, I was mildly startled at the sight of two enormous bruises at the tops of my thighs where the harness buckles had dug in. The most impressive bruise measured about six inches by four and did little to enhance an already sorry looking aged thigh. The bath was bliss, but the water carried a fairly potent whiff of sulphur. Refreshed I ordered a Caesar salad and a beer and ended the day with a phone call home.

Later to bed than usual, I couldn't sleep and wasn't sure if it was too much sun or the last rumblings of ladder fright. Whatever the reason sleep eventually won the battle but when I awoke, it was to the rhythmic throbbing of a sun-induced headache. Another stumble past the mirror revealed a large radiating cold sore. So now I would meet Matt and Alice complete with suppurating sore. I had one when I last saw them at Christmas (festive stress), so they'll probably think it's a permanent feature.

Friday 5th April: sulphurous smells and Maori memorabilia

I well remember the day of sulphur, silica and sinter and of course Lady Knox. Up at daybreak and on the road by eight-thirty to enjoy a lovely drive through forests and mountains down to the thermal wonderland that is Wai-O-Tapu.

On arrival discovered that the Lady Knox geyser was a short detour from the main thermal area and so with time in hand, I walked around the slurping, burping, smelly sulphurous pools, with names like champagne pool, frying pan flat and mud pool. The colours were extraordinary, such a range in a relatively small area; all the colours of the rainbow appeared to be present and correct, from a pretty primrose yellow hued sulphur to the deep red-brown of iron oxide, plus the black of carbon and more sulphur – this time at the opposite end of the yellow spectrum from its delicate floral cousin.

In awe of nature's simmering energy, I sauntered back to the car in readiness for my appointed rendezvous. Up to this point I had been fairly much on my own, but by the time I reached the geyser car park, most of North Island seemed to have joined me. The attendant giving directions promised me a sight to remember and genially beamed with enthusiasm for Wai-O-Tapu and all its magical pools. From what I had already seen, I didn't doubt him.

As instructed, I found my seat and sat staring at the docile looking white cone that was Lady Knox, waiting for the action. With minutes still to spare, I browsed my information leaflet and read that volcanic activity in the region dated back approximately 15,000 years. The thermal area covers some 18 square kilometres of which only a small portion is seen by tourists. Thinking about my meander amongst Beelzebub's cauldrons, possibly the reason for areas being out of bounds to a wandering public is the combined challenge presented by the sheer number of collapsed craters, the abundance of sinter-edged pools of boiling mud and water as well as the numerous steaming gas emitting fumaroles. Trying to weave safe walkways through all that thermal activity would present a health and safety nightmare.

Focusing my attention back on the cone, the chap from the car park morphed from car park attendant into geyser guide as he re-appeared and poured something into the void of Lady Knox. Ah ha! So that's the secret. Soap! Soap breaks the water's surface tension, which is why, bang on cue at ten-fifteen off she blows. A few minutes of dribbling and drooling precede the main event, but when it happens, a fifteen metre flume of water, erupts skywards to the *oohing* and *aahing* of the massed ranks of spectators. Apparently, if left to Mother Nature, the geyser would have a twenty-four to forty-eight hour cycle which would be a bit tricky to manage as a money spinner. I didn't think to ask if consequently the naturally occurring plume of water would be any larger. I guess it would. Lady Knox's dramatic reaction to soap was discovered by accident. The geyser is on a site that was once a penal colony and for some reason the prisoners tipped soapy water into the cone and bingo up she went and a money spinner was born.

A guy in the audience, another lone traveller, asked me to take a photo of him with the erupting Lady Knox in the background, I obliged and he then returned the honour, saying. "That'll be a great shot". Have now seen the result – my very excited face appears at the bottom of the photo with a massive steamy blur above and behind me, which looks very odd indeed. Not a great one for the album. I hope my effort on his behalf was better.

After a few more minutes of *oohing* and *aahing*, the crowds dispersed and I followed on having lingered a little longer at one of nature's awe-inspiring sites. The cheerful multi-tasking geyser chap caught up with me and we chatted about the park and Lady Knox. After several years of giving breakfast to her three times a week, he still finds it a truly amazing experience. He loves the thermal park with its rainbow colours. We enthused about the phenomenon of the champagne pool with its various oxides and fabulous water with teeny, tiny bubbles… just like champagne!

Bidding farewell I returned to the main thermal area and opted for the long walk to ensure that I saw everything that tourists were allowed to see. Inevitably I took masses of photos, most of which do no justice to the splendour of the burping, bubbling, slurping, steaming, smelly sulphur pools nor the limestone caves and caverns. Possibly if geological surveys are your thing, you'd gain something from looking at my handiwork, and probably you'd know which way was up… as I certainly don't. Sadly my knowledge is limited to the coloured elements I like, such as the striking purple of manganese oxide. I guess my geological photos will just gather domestic dust when back at home.

Irrespective of my photographic prowess, I left the park in a very happy mood at about one-thirty to head back towards Hamilton. As the weather was clouding over, I was not really sure what I wanted to do but had noticed a 'Maori village' on the way down and wondered if it was worth a visit. As I approached I thought, 'Might as well,' but was a bit dubious as it was probably a tacky tourist attraction… and was that what the indigenous people really wanted as a memorial to their past? Without any great air of expectation, I paid my money and had a twenty minute wait before the next tour. I spent the time looking at a motley selection of souvenirs in the Maori arts and crafts village and began to regret my fifteen dollar entrance fee.

The minutes ticked by when, along with a few fellow stragglers, we were peremptorily summoned by a Rarotongan-reminiscent blast from a conch shell and ushered through a stockade by our Maori guide. And a very interesting forty-five minutes followed. No bad white guy stuff, not even a sub-text (although I think that might have been understandable/justifiable) but all about how the Maori people had lived pre-colonisation. Warfare was a calendar event. When there was nothing else to do, they fought – mainly over women and land. They seemed to have had an aggressive streak which flared up with little provocation. Learnt about the painful tribal markings and the games they played to strengthen their wrist action to optimise the efficacy of their weapons, especially the spatulate *mere* made from green jade or *patu* made from wood. A well aimed swipe from one of these could take the top off a skull like taking the top off a boiled egg; all very graphic. Really enjoyed a highly informative and fun visit! It was worth every cent. Although very different, the two activities of the day had been a great success. Part of the joy of this journey is encountering the unexpected – and the Maori village proved the point. In future I won't quibble over the price of an entry ticket.

Back on the road and Hamilton the next stop. The drive was uneventful, wet, and a bit boring as I had already navigated this stretch before. On arriving back again in town I discovered that there was a ballooning event taking place; good, this should liven things up a little. Found the hotel and checked in to the inappropriately named Le Grand and went for a stroll. Had the usual 'bun and coffee' late lunch at about five. Not sure what had happened to the balloons, no sign of life skywards or town-wise. Regret to say I didn't warm to Hamilton second time round any more than I had on my first visit, but it was only a night stop before Sydney, so anything was going to be bearable.

Writing this I have just had a thought… perhaps introspection is an odd mood I'm slipping into on my own. Possibly it's fuelled by the contrast between having a fantastic, interesting and exciting day interspersed with conversation followed by mooching silently around a very quiet town. *Who knows?*

In my room I raided the mini-bar and caught up with journal writing and so managed to miss dinner. Bed by ten-ish, just as Friday night was finally hotting up. Plus, I had some very noisy Italians in the next room – one of whom thought he was Pavarotti, so I settled back thinking sleep might be a luxury. I was right. Unfortunately my room overlooked the main street by a set of traffic lights and the late night noise of revving engines and pounding music from cars waiting for the green light just didn't stop. All night I drifted in and out of sleep finally falling into a deep slumber at about five... only to be awoken at six on the dot as the municipal clean-up team rolled into action. Needed to be up early, so not really a problem. So that was that.

And what had I written about Hamilton being a quiet town?

Sydney and a family reunion

Saturday 6th April: Sydney, Matt and Alice – at last!

The day started with a mediocre breakfast, but excitement rather than calories would be fuelling my day. Left the hotel without a backward glance and hit the city limits at eight-fifteen… next stop Auckland.

Arrived back at Auckland airport in good time, before ten, in pouring rain and dropped off the car with a bit of a sad goodbye as I had enjoyed clocking up my 1434km or 891 miles. On reflection, that doesn't seem like a lot of driving… *Have I got this wrong?*

The good start to the day halted abruptly when I was greeted by mayhem in the check-in area. Went and had a drink and daren't say what to eat (little else to choose from – how did the world manage pre-muffin?) and then finally braced myself for the check-in queue. Post my Heathrow departure, security had been nothing more than the norm… up until this point. As my small bag bounced its way through the x-ray machine, I was almost leapt upon by a security chap. Complacency shattered, there then followed a brief but intense discussion as to how much damage to life and limb could be inflicted by my very small tweezers. I won the debate. After that, all was thankfully uneventful but I have now developed an almost magnetic

71

attraction towards security staff, virtually running at bewildered officers – arms akimbo. Unsurprisingly, the randomness of searches now seems a little less random when applied to me.

As the plane climbed up and away from the receding seventy-one islands of Auckland's bay I remembered the anxious couple from Derbyshire. Had they made contact with their children? Was the news good? Had they been able to stop fretting and enjoy the remainder of their holiday? Alas I would never know. Nourished by my third meal of the day, a surprisingly tasty in-flight cheese and ham ciabatta, I decided that ruminating over unanswerable puzzles obviously encouraged an appetite.

In brilliant sunshine, and with my excitement levels rising, we finally touched down in Sydney where a sunny Matt and Alice waited to greet me. The exuberance of their welcome confirmed that they were well, happy and enjoying their new lifestyle. Wonderful! I tried to be mature about this reunion and not let the side down with sobs of maternal joy, but perhaps a few tears are permissible on such occasions. Then, as currently car-less, in a battered borrowed car with George crammed into the boot with no room for waltzing, they whizzed me off on a grand tour of the city sights and sites involving much to-ing and fro-ing over the majestic and rightly iconic Harbour Bridge. Known locally as the Coathanger Bridge because of its arch shape, the 'coathanger' provides a splendid piece of architecture from which to suspend the New Year celebratory fireworks: a happy outcome. However, I doubt if that criterion was presented to the designer of the steel arch, Sir Ralph Freeman.

The Coathanger... from which to suspend celebratory fireworks...

We finally parked and took a stroll overlooking one of the many bays which make Sydney harbour so spectacular. Saw my first golden orb spider (very large) and a graceful tree with bright purple flowers, species unknown to my hosts, but since identified as the Jacaranda tree.

Enjoyed a welcome glass or two of beer at Watsons Bay Hotel and watched the sun sink over the dramatic Sydney skyline, then headed back to Yurong Street and their home. A gated entrance leads into a tiny courtyard and then into a charming and characterful house which, with its three bedrooms and two bathrooms, makes it an ideal house for two couples to share, this they do with Damon and Odette. Had a glass of wine and a chat and then off to a tremendous restaurant, Lisa's, just around the corner on Stanley Street for a welcome muffin-free supper of barramundi and garlic mash and, of course, more wine.

Can't remember going to bed, but I suppose I did.

Sunday 7th April: getting my bearings

After the rain of New Zealand, the sunshine of Oz continued. First thing, took a brief amble around nearby streets and saw rows of delightful Victorian workers' cottages with their wrought iron balconies, had no idea that such pretty houses existed in and around Sydney. When first built, these tiny houses lacked sanitation and their cheek by jowl proximity provided no defence against the bubonic plague which romped through areas of Sydney close to the harbour in the 1900s. Looking at these now contemporary dwellings, I was impressed by the ingenious ways they had been extended, it showed a sympathetic and imaginative approach to today's planning process. UK planners, please take note.

Thinking my architectural appreciation was temporarily suspended, we headed off to Balmoral Beach for breakfast in the old Bathers' Pavilion. The snaking queue signalled that this was an immensely popular venue and our patience was rewarded when we finally got a table, magically, with a sea view. Tucking into indulgently rich eggs Benedict, I understood why this was a place worth queuing for: delicious. Mopping up the last of my eggy crumbs, I mused that this was another innovative piece of architectural renovation. Built in the 1920s as a changing 'shed' it had been structurally enhanced in 1929 with a mix of art deco and Moorish influences: my architectural appreciation was still in full swing.

Heading back to the house, we dropped Alice off at the historic Queen Victoria Building to buy picnic basics from the sumptuous food hall. This superb Romanesque edifice was commissioned at the end of the 19th century to provide out-of-work craftsmen with employment during a time of recession, and the building today stands as a testament to their enduring skills. If my time in New Zealand was epitomised by what I saw inside the buildings, such as in the eclectic museums, here in Sydney I was fascinated by the external mix of the old and the new.

A quick zap around the house to gather up bits and pieces and off we set to meet friends on a cliff top overlooking the harbour... from a different angle. It was a lovely grassy spot, with no one else around, just our party: an idyllic lazy Sunday afternoon. Excellent crowd and everyone made me feel very welcome. If not joining in the conversation, then what could be a better sedentary activity than watching the balletic watery activity of dozens of small (and some not so small) sailing boats going 'ready about – lee ho' in the waters of the harbour? Bliss to watch and I expect bliss to do.

Eventually the evening chill sent each party off in different directions and Judy, the owner of our borrowed wheels, reclaimed her car. Can't believe how generous everyone is with their possessions. Was sorry to say good-bye to New Zealand but I'm loving every minute of Sydney. Already beginning to understand why my son's round-the-world ticket is only 50 percent utilised.

Sadly, the day had been marred by a phone call from Odette saying that she and Damon had disturbed an intruder in the Yurong Street house, which was an understandably unsettling experience. Although the front of the house is secure, the back is overlooked by a lodging house and a service alley runs parallel to the back fence. The fence is quite high, but the uninvited guest had hopped over without too much difficulty, as his retreating rear demonstrated. Bikes and clothes had mysteriously disappeared from the yard in the past, possibly liberated by the same nimble limbed person whose interpretation towards being generous with possessions was obviously diametrically opposed to Judy's.

Unperturbed by the intruder incident, Odette cooked pasta with tomato sauce and Alice tossed a healthy fresh green salad (my muffin days are over). Again, must have hit the pillow at some stage – but have no memory of my head connecting with my bed.

How spooky! Just as I was writing about the intruder in Yurong Street, someone was trying to get into my hotel room in Melbourne and they were being a tad persistent. "Ah, solly..." a lost Japanese tourist, I guessed. I later discovered that he had stayed previously at the hotel and regarded room 225 as his.

Monday 8th April: bearings still not 'got'

And still the sun shines. Monday, so it must be washing day. On my own from 8am and rather pleased that the intruder didn't reappear whilst I busied myself with the top loader and draped wet clothes around my room. Also took it upon myself to helpfully tidy a kitchen cupboard, an action which continues to vex my son to this day... he had cleaned the cupboard in anticipation of my arrival: *ouch*. As midday approached I set off to meet Matt for lunch and got totally lost in the Surry Hills area (still can't get used to that weird spelling). Shouldn't have been anywhere near there, so not quite sure what went wrong and the A-Z was no help at all. Found a bus stop with a bench in the hope that a calm approach to map-reading would clarify matters, but after several minutes I was still none the wiser re my whereabouts.

A chap from JC Decaux (of the advertising hoardings) who had been sitting on the pavement reading *The Easter Stories*, asked if I was waiting for a bus. "No, lost," I said. "Ah, I always get lost," came his none too positive reply. He then added that I might find his mini map easier to interpret. It was. He pointed me in the right direction and with his gifted map in hand, soon found myself down by Darling Harbour and then crossed over the Pyrmont Bridge to the other shore. I just hope that the kind gentleman from JC Decaux, now parted from his map, was not circling the Surry Hills looking for a way home.

In a few minutes Matt arrived and showed me his office location. What a place to work! Standing one block back from the water, the building is set at an angle to provide harbour views for the incarcerated workers. Daydream heaven! The area is busy with the hustle and bustle of tourists and workers all rubbing shoulders creating a vibrant location – a location that is considerably better than the one I enjoyed at City Road in London. We tucked into a Japanese lunch to get me in training for next month's trip to see number two child, Kate, at her place of work in Tokyo. (*Aha*, I'm not totally selfish as I'll be joined on that leg of my journey by my husband.) Obviously, the upside of having itinerant children is all the foreign travel required to catch up with them. The downsides are the dwindling pension pot and the wobbly bottom lip every time we part; it should get easier to say "bye for now" but it doesn't. Sorry, that's a maternal digression...

Returning to number one child – said "cheerio" to the worker and went back across the surprisingly long Pyrmont Bridge, with its overhead monorail, an Olympics legacy, and spent two happy hours visiting the Sydney aquarium. Terrific shark and stingray tank, which was being cleaned whilst some of the inmates were being distracted with food. The two metre sharks seemed quite unconcerned by the men in masks swimming amongst them, just as nonplussed as the men themselves seemed to be in the presence of lots of pearly white teeth. Then spent an absolute age watching a busy, busy duck-billed platypus, he was quite mesmerising swimming backwards and forwards scooping up small fish in his bill. They must have been his lunch, but it looked as if he was just re-arranging them... placing a batch here and another over there... busy, busy.

Back over the bridge again to collect photos of the first part of my trip and had a cuppa to make sure I had enough energy to go... back over the ever-lengthening bridge to the aquarium where I caught the ferry to Circular Quay and the Opera House. Time for only a brief look at the outside of the Opera House, Sydney's second iconic structure (will have to go back) before heading inland via The Domain for home, which is on the far side of the familiarly named (and spelt) Hyde Park.

Quick round of phone calls home and a bit of spit and polish and then off to Davinda's for veggie curry and to watch the film *Lantana* with Geoffrey Rush; it's set in the Sydney suburbs and deals with that age-old trinity of love, sex and deceit. No seats, audience just lounges on cushions – except for Matt and me, no more cushions so we sat primly on plastic chairs looking like a couple of cinema ushers. Extremely good film and a really excellent evening, I'm beginning to feel rather at home in Sydney.

Again, must have gone to bed, but too tired to notice, although at some stage did manage to cram lots of still soggy clothes into George in preparation for Melbourne tomorrow before the start of my Great Ocean Road adventure.

Melbourne in double-quick time

Tuesday 9th April: back on my own and off to Melbourne

Trundled George down to the main road to hail a cab for the airport and check in ahead of the business crowd. By ten was seated on a virtually full 767 alongside a motley mix of unwashed back packers and perfumed city slickers. An hour and five minutes later we landed – heavily – in Melbourne. Caught the Skybus into town and then a minibus to the hotel; an excellent system. Found myself checking into (a little sheepishly) an elegant Radisson hotel, in an ideal location on Flagstaff Gardens which is just on the edge of the Central Business District, where most of Melbourne life happens. Managed a quick wash and brush up and hung up the still soggy clothes, using cupboard doors, curtain rails and any accommodating surface thereby changing my lovely room into something resembling a doss-house. Satisfied with the transformation, then went off to explore, walking for miles and miles with an attractive cold sore throbbing (my Sydney hosts had been far too polite to draw attention to my pustule, but we did do a lot of air kisses).

Planned and executed my 'see Melbourne in less than a day' itinerary as follows:

- Swanston Street for the Edwardian baroque city baths, Neo-classical state library and the modern architecture of the museum. Then strolled to the...
- Gothic transitional architecture of St Paul's Anglican Cathedral, on to the...
- Renaissance Revival of the Regent theatre plus other assorted theatres I stumbled across. Decided to up my speed and headed for the...
- Edwardian baroque of Flinders Street railway station with its beautiful art deco glass windows. Having reached its centenary, this red brick and stucco Melbourne landmark, crowned with a dome, hints at the confidence and glories of a bygone era. How many railway stations today boast a ballroom? Such a prestigious building is indicative of the role played by the railways in the growth of the city and its suburbs. Suitably informed and impressed, without drawing breath...
- Parliament area for the Gothic Revival of St Patrick's Roman Catholic cathedral. Here I sat (gratefully) and watched the warm amber glow of the afternoon sun as it seeped in through the windows. Next...
- Fitzroy Gardens where, tucked away, is the cottage in which Captain Cook's parents once lived... in England. Revived flagging energy bubbles with a drink and a poppy seed biscuit, before heading...
- South of the Yarra for the landscaped loveliness of the Royal Botanic Gardens. It was here that I realised what gems the Australian botanical gardens are. To do it justice requires up to three hours at a gentle amble. Then, was I feeling jaded or...
- Did I close my eyes passing the glory of the Queen Victoria

Market and similarly the Neo-classical architecture of the
State Parliament House? I have no note of either but hard
to miss as so large and striking. Onwards towards the…

- Victorian Artists Society – Victorian as in Victoria, Australia
not circa 1850, but housed in a Victorian building circa 1850
– all very confusing. And then unforgettably…
- The morbidly gruesome but Old Melbourne Gaol with its
Art of Hanging exhibition and the stuff of nightmares. In the
museum's own words:

The Old Melbourne Gaol offers a chilling insight into
prison life. In 1841, after six years of European settlement
the increasing lawlessness necessitated the building
of a gaol to accommodate short-term prisoners, those
on remand, those accused of minor offences such as
drunkenness, lunacy, vagrancy or bankruptcy and those
awaiting execution.

Within ten years it was struggling to accommodate
the increasing number of prisoners and so a second wing
was added based on the Model Prison at Pentonville,
London. Architecture was used as part of the process
of social reform. Prisoners were incarcerated not only
from the outside world but from each other, in single
solitary cells, thus enabling a strict rule of silence to be
enforced. Corporal punishment was meted out via the
lashing triangle or the cat 'o' nine tails and prisoners were
required to wear calico hoods when they left their cells.

The Melbourne Gaol was the scene of 135 hangings,
including that of the infamous bushranger, Ned Kelly:
the scaffold on which he was hanged survives. The Gaol
houses a grim yet fascinating collection of death masks
of executed prisoners, including that of Ned Kelly. These
were used in the scientific study of phrenology in order
to understand the criminal mind.[4]

As I said, unforgettable and it did send a shiver down my spine: *brrr.*

And finally to a sublime setting on Collins Street where, as a reward for galloping around Melbourne's tourist trail, I downed a much-needed cool beer. Shoes off, legs sprawled, I sat lazily watching as city workers scurried past homeward bound. Syphoning the dregs, I reluctantly heaved myself up to join the apparent exodus. Virtually crawled my way back to the hotel where, overcome by exhaustion, I burst into tears when I phoned home. My companionable cold sore was really getting me down. Did some therapeutic hand-washing and ironing… *Would genuine backpackers reach for an iron?* Probably not, but then they wouldn't be staying in the Radisson would they? Craving sustenance I ordered a beef sandwich and watched the Queen Mother's funeral on the telly. Pottered and pottered and collapsed into bed too tired to think.

Wednesday 10th April: sorry, but more sun – how lovely!

Having given my legs a strenuous workout yesterday, caught the free circle line tram around to Flinders Street station to check out the booking hall at a more leisurely pace. Side-stepping passengers, I photographed the ornate art deco window above the arched entrance and decided that it could really do with a bit of a clean. Fortunately, the grime could not totally camouflage the delicate beauty of the glass. Trains have been pulling up at the platforms on this site since 1854 and today's rail service provider, Connex, has a very prominent Customer Charter which promises to improve service and punctuality. I wonder, is this Connex the same as ours? If so, could we have similar promises which it then keeps? Please? [Back at home I caught up with the demise of the UK train service provider, which sort of answered my questions].

Bought a tram day pass and wandered over to St Paul's Cathedral to take a closer look. To my inexpert eye, the Gothic architecture acted as a striking reminder of the ancestral roots of the Victorian settlers. The high altar with its gilt mosaic reredos, reminded me of the altar in Butterfield's Gothic All Saints, Margaret Street, London. Even the organ pipes were spectacular; they looked like a bank of sharpened pencils, all painstakingly decorated and neatly lined up waiting for the hand of a giant scribe. Chatted to the ladies at the souvenir stall and bought four postcards, a choice and transaction which met with their approval. Switching from all things ecclesiastical to the royal family, they said how impressed they had been by the Queen Mother's funeral. They had especially enjoyed seeing a bird's eye view of Westminster Abbey during yesterday's service, as it reminded them of their visit to the Abbey on a recent trip to England. Nodding in synchronised duck-like fashion, we all agreed that Britain's fabled excellence at mastering pomp and ceremony was no false claim.

Pleasantries over, it was back out onto St Kilda's Road to catch the Number 8 tram to the Botanic Gardens for more areas of fabulousness. Spent a tranquil time wandering amidst the Titans of the tree-world, on which were suspended and upended smelly fruit bats looking like the devil's decorations. I sauntered beside ponds, strode across springy grass and admired plants of every size, shape and hue. Set against a backdrop of the city's skyscrapers, this is somewhere I could have lingered longer. Instead, it has been added to my growing list of places to (re) visit on a future occasion.

But time marches on… so off to find the Number 16 tram for St Kilda's Beach and then alighted before the route terminated to walk down to the sea front. Must find some more imaginative adjectives, but again quite 'fabulous'. A shared pedestrian, cycle, skater path runs for as far as the eye can see both east and west. Plus, *slip, slap, slop.* Everywhere I go (and not just in Melbourne) I seem to have swarms of small children swamped beneath very large hats buzzing around my knees, and all around there are posters reminding everyone to *slip, slap, slop* on the sunscreen. As I strolled along, batting these walking hats out of my way, I wished that I had brought my cossie and therefore, understandably, felt the need to console myself with an ice cream. Sat by the sea feeling at peace with the world and telephoned Matt to tell him so.

... Swarms of small children swamped beneath very large hats...

Energised by a temporary sugar-rush, I headed towards the marina which was a tiny blur on the eastern horizon. Here I mooched around admiring lots of lovely boats whilst serenaded by the gentle jangle of halyards tapping against gently rocking masts. With a salty sigh of farewell, I decided (mistakenly) not to retrace my steps, opting instead to just keep going. After a little while I began to feel the call of nature and realised that I had left all buildings behind. Scanning the distant vista, there wasn't even the smallest of bushes to offer twig-like privacy, just (seemingly) miles of open road edged by a grass verge along which enough people were scattered to deter me from throwing caution to the wind. Finally I hit a main road and crossed into a residential area where, joy of joys and in the nick of time, I found a pizza parlour. Phew! Panic over, I settled down to enjoy a cheese and tomato laden slice of pizza, a green salad and a mug of coffee all for an unbelievable $5.20 – worth every cent in more ways than one!

Before I continue, I just have to express how hard it can be to convey the timely weirdness of some of my discoveries. For instance, the pizza parlour was a one-off as there were no other shops nearby. It was as if I had wished for relief and sustenance and *abracadabra* there it was in all its homely glory. It could so easily have been a video shop... or nothing at all...

Anyway, feeling relieved and replete, I headed north for thirty minutes or so and, from a location 3km east of St Kilda, finally found the 67 tram back into town. Disembarked at Chinatown and realised that I was strolling past a sort of twilight red light district – naked girls and happy Buddhas marked my alternate steps; a great place to food shop. I then wandered into the Greek precinct to be met by 'give us back our marbles' posters and lots of gooey cakes in an assortment of coffee shops, but they failed to lure me in. Meandered back towards the hotel and knew I was in the right area when the majority of the pedestrians were bewigged and gowned; the hotel is near the courts of law.

Back in my clothes-strewn room, I flopped on to the bed and did a crossword puzzle, had a beer, caught up with my journal and ordered a meal. Thinking it honourable to be frugal, it was the cheapest item on the menu and now I know why, as most of it is sitting uneaten outside my bedroom door: yuk, yuk. The Eastern Feast was nothing but bean sprouts swimming in warm oil: again, yuk, yuk. Still, so far the food in Oz has been terrific, better than New Zealand, where I might have been unlucky as I didn't really sample any local cooking, what I ate was all a bit touristy. Perhaps with the exception of my stainless steel canteen meal, which wasn't really on the main tourist trail – I guess.

You may have gathered by now, that after a day of sightseeing I usually wend my way back to my hotel and rarely venture out in the evening. I don't mind eating alone in the hours of daylight, but only occasionally do I sally forth at night. Not really sure why. Anyway, tomorrow is the start of the Great Ocean Road adventure, so it's time to iron the last of my laundry and climb into bed.

One more quick thought, I'm not sure that I have been very good at describing my impressions of the places I have visited, so to atone... Melbourne is welcoming, attractive and accessible. There are lots of Victorian Gothic buildings and fewer high rise office blocks than Sydney and more space between buildings. Obviously it's much smaller than Sydney, but the echoes of the superior role it once played are far from faint. Have only seen the central area, but there appears to be a greater concentration of wealth in the city, with fewer signs of homeless people or vagrants clutching beer cans than might be seen in its New South Wales counterpart. I'm sure all cities have their dark underbelly but my Melbourne eyes only saw a comely sense of order.

Not sure that recording my thoughts sounds anything other than pretentious, so in more simplistic terms it is quite simply a lovely city which is, I reiterate, welcoming, attractive and accessible. These are all good visitor attributes for a girl going solo.

Pen down, journal away, lights out... I really do have a busy day ahead of me.

Off to Adelaide via the Great Ocean Road

Thursday 11th April: and off we go, planned itinerary as follows...

... northwest to Ballarat and Sovereign Hill for tales of the gold rush, the botanic gardens and then south to Geelong, Torquay, Bells Beach, the lighthouse at Aireys Inlet, Point Addis with spectacular views and the beguiling town of Lorne.

Trundled George round to Franklin Street, thankfully not too far away, to collect my car, where I found I had been given an upgrade at no extra cost from a small manual lawn mower to a large bright red automatic Mitsubishi Lancer. Once again a free upgrade and once again George had room to roam. Navigated my way out of Melbourne and realised that I was on the wrong road, having got wedged between two huge lorries thereby missing the left filter to Ballarat I was now on my way, erroneously, to Geelong. A quick buzz up and down one motorway soon had me back on the Ballarat road: Geelong comes later. When not scanning upwards for road signs, scanning down I was amazed to see two sheep dogs being carried in a container set between the wheels of a sheep transporter at axle height. They barked at all vehicles drawing up alongside at traffic lights and seemed only a whiskery snarl away from escaping their mobile confines. You don't see that on London's South Circular.

... You don't see that on London's South Circular...

Not only is Melbourne home to weird forms of animal transportation, it is also home to the novelty of 'hook turns'. My route out of town was not all about turning left and as I approached my first right manoeuvre, I did so with some trepidation hoping that I wasn't going to be at the head of the right-turning queue: fortunately I wasn't. The manoeuvre is designed to keep turning traffic away from the central section of an intersection, and occurs when you have a tramline on your right. Therefore, when turning right, you approach the turn from the nearside lane of the road you're on then proceed straight over the intersection to the point where you 'hook' right, at the last possible moment. It's less complicated than it sounds as these junctions are traffic light controlled – otherwise there would be absolute carnage.

Ninety minutes in the car on a blistering day and I arrived at Ballarat and found my way to the tourist attraction of Sovereign Hill. This is the actual site of the main 1850s gold/quartz mine which has been recreated as a mining village circa the days of the gold rush. Far from being tacky, it was extremely good and highly informative. I learnt that the largest contingent of prospectors, from amongst several thousand in total, had come from China. An estimated 40,000 Chinese worked systematically and diligently gathering the alluvial gold from the gravel of buried creeks. They often continued to work on sites abandoned by European and American prospectors and their subsequent success fuelled animosity. To defuse the situation, the Chinese were 'taxed' for protection by European officials, Protectors.

Having spent time underground in New Zealand, I couldn't resist going underground here. I ventured down two mines, including Red Hill which had a weirdly realistic hologram of the man who found the world's second largest gold nugget, the Welcome Nugget. Spent much longer at the open air museum than anticipated, but still only saw or took part in half of the activities available. There is also a gold museum on the opposite side of the road, but the information didn't add to anything to what I had already learnt from my two mine trips.

I omitted to note, and have therefore forgotten, the technicalities of extracting the gold-bearing quartz. In contrast, the conditions in which the miners worked were appalling and so remain indelibly etched upon my memory. For many the rewards for dangerous and sweaty work were scant, so it must have been the prospect of making it rich... which kept them prospecting. There is still a lot of gold in the quartz in the surrounding area and it is again being mined, but water seepage had halted mining at Sovereign Hill until technology solved the problem.

Visit over, downed a cuppa and a melting moment (a buttery shortbread biscuit which seems to be a Victorian speciality) and set off once more for the 243km route that is the Great Ocean Road. My onboard musings led to my decision that the use of the word 'Victorian' is very confusing... my expectations got muddled more than once when something seemingly associated with a deceased monarch, related to the very much alive and well state of Victoria – either way, the 19th-century architecture is glorious and what I have seen of the 21st-century state, it is a treat. Sadly there was no time for

Ballarat's Fine Art Gallery nor the lake and Botanic Gardens. More for that ever-growing list...

Once again Geelong featured on my navigational route. At Geelong the main road heads west inland, and it's a minor road that goes down to and along the coast. As ever, I got lost and therefore lost all sight of helpful road signs, but by trial and error and a good circumnavigation of the Geelong suburbs (what a lot of bungalows), found the road I was looking for. I didn't have a map, which probably didn't help matters. I pootled down to the sea and the famous surfing beaches of Torquay and Bells Beach, followed by a dusty drive out to the remote Aireys Inlet where stands the gleaming Split Point lighthouse. Known, appropriately, as the White Queen, the lighthouse shines its beacon to aid vessels rounding Cape Otway. Although it was getting towards dusk and I wasn't sure where I was staying, I decided that there was time to troop swiftly up the hill to greet one more lighthouse, an especially majestic one. On my way back to the car I glanced out over the sea, and then along the coastline to where several people, looking like penguins in their wetsuits, were making the most of what surf there was. It was a good decision to linger; the warm herb-perfumed air was a perfect antidote to time spent behind the wheel of the Lancer.

My travels for the day ended at Lorne and I pulled into the weirdly uneven car park of the Grand Pacific Hotel, a guide book recommendation which came with the warning that it had passed its prime but had spectacular views. A very seedy bloke eventually shuffled out from behind a curtain to loom over the reception desk and said, in answer to my question, that it would be '160 dollars' for a room. With a squeaky reply of, "No thank you," I retreated and then bounced the car out across the lunar landscape to drive back into town to the Lorne Hotel. Driving past earlier it hadn't struck me as ideal as the bottle shop and pokies (one-armed bandits) seemed to dominate, but it was getting late and dark and I was tired. Just had a thought, perhaps

I owe the bloke at the Grand Pacific an apology as he might have thought that I looked seedy as I'm still sporting the mother of all cold sores.

With low expectations, I checked in for 100 dollars and found myself in a delightful room, with a wonderful view overlooking the sea and the smell of fresh new paint as it had just been refurbished. Flopping down, I surveyed my surroundings and decided that this was a room I could call home; the cane furniture on which I had plonked my weary self gave it an unexpectedly colonial Somerset Maugham feel. Although the room was memorable, the supper I then tucked into in the hotel's bistro, wasn't. Not finished with the day, I then retreated to the bar where I sat happily sipping and reading. Returning to my room, I caught the end of an Oxfam fundraiser on television; it was a tie-in to the Melbourne Comedy Month, with assorted comedians from around the world each doing a four minute slot. Some of the acts were very funny indeed and the programme made realise that I hadn't laughed out loud for ages… fortunately my cackling laughter was drowned out by the sound of heavy rain pounding on the roof.

The sound of breaking surf and thrashing rain combined to create a perfect lullaby, which even the regular *kerchink, kerchink* of the pokies could not spoil.

Friday 12th April: the journey continues as follows…

Apollo Bay for a spot of sandy relaxation; Otway rain forest; Shipwreck coast; Moonlight head; the slightly reduced Twelve Apostles with London Bridge; Loch Ard Gorge; Port Campbell; Peterborough; Warrnambool for an optimistic spot of whale watching; Port Fairy, pretty in both name and nature; Portland; Mount Gambier where the cobalt Blue Lake… is steel grey in April. Mileage-wise, *a tad ambitious perhaps*?

The rain continued throughout the night, but it was fun because of its enormity. In the morning, I wandered briefly around a surprisingly dry Lorne, where I ate a truly Australian breakfast of raisin toast sitting outside a roadside café. It seemed that most of the town, all looking hail, hearty and windswept with surfboards attached to their wrists, as if waiting for a wave to scoot along the pavement, ambled by eyeing my toast hungrily. Wanting to linger in this delightful spot a little longer but knowing that a full day lay ahead, I reluctantly bid farewell to Lorne.

The next scheduled stop was Apollo Bay. The scenic coastline route to my destination is described in tourist blurb as 'one of the most beautiful and breathtaking drives in the world' so I decided to first look down upon it by taking a detour slightly inland to Mariners Lookout, which, unsurprisingly, required a hill climb. Almost got to the top when I was overcome by an attack of the heeby jeebies; it was an isolated spot and there was no one else around. I took a few hasty photos from 'almost' the top and then trotted nimbly back down to the car park. Another car now took up a second slot, parked too close to mine for comfort. To get into the driver's seat, I had to enter via the passenger door and scrabble in an ungainly fashion over the gear stick. Fortunately, I guess, there was no sign of the second vehicle's occupant, which was odd as I had been on the only footpath. My sleuthing vibes decided it must be occupant singular, because unless their passenger had a penchant for climbing over gear sticks, they too would have faced an ingress/egress dilemma like mine: *just a tiny bit strange don't you think*?

Out onto the road to continue the scenic drive and by the time I drifted into Apollo Bay, with its glorious stretch of sandy beach, my palpitations had subsided. I rewarded my bravery with an ice cream, which didn't quite match the deliciousness of the one I'd enjoyed on the sea front at St Kilda... so that's ice creams done for this holiday. The anticipated sugar rush was welcome, though!

The Great Ocean Road is steep and twisty from this point on, with more breathtaking views. My journey naturally included several stops to take pictures or just to stand and look. Had a scamper on the sands at Wye River Bay where I played with a gigantic piece of kelp and then wrote the wrong date in the sand: I had lost track of time... and my inhibitions. The road then veers inland at a small peninsular which is the Otway Rain Forest – just a tiny piece of unspoiled rain forest. This was one of those rare occasions when I would have enjoyed having a partner with me so that together we could walk deep into the forest. Sorry, the yearning for a partner was not a romantic whimsy, simply all about 'safety in numbers' after my Mariners Lookout wobble. However, I did venture for a short distance into the midst of the beckoning trees and was greeted by strange sounds and the wonderful smell of forest myrtle. Was entranced by the variety of gum trees which either looked dishevelled and unkempt, as papery bark peeled off in long dazzling strips, or smooth as smooth can be with bright shiny trunks soaring up into the canopy. Would really love to go back, but next time would be prepared with long socks as leeches and tics are common.

Took a 24km detour to see the Cape Otway lightstation and on the way passed a road sign warning of cows, koalas, kangaroos and... pterodactyls. Can't think what they were meant to be, perhaps an attempt at drawing a pelican in flight, several of which I had seen but usually bobbing up and down on water. The scenery changed as the vegetation thinned out and then the road petered out, but finally arrived at the lighthouse and was pleased to have made the effort. Climbed to the top for a stunning sea view and chatted to the guide before retracing my steps via a very handy portaloo in the middle of a field. I'm not sure if it was meant for agricultural workers or tourists, either way I was grateful for the facility: another example of 'timely weirdness'. Talking to the guide, I learnt that:

- The Cape Otway Lightstation is the oldest surviving lighthouse on the Australian mainland. It was built in 1848, and, with Cape Wickham lighthouse on King Island, marks the entrance to the Bass Strait.
- The light, which was originally fuelled by whale oil and later by kerosene, diesel and finally electricity, shone 40km out to sea. In 1994 the 'Old Light' was decommissioned and replaced with a solar powered beacon which is positioned directly in front of the sandstone lighthouse.

Even in remote spots you find erudite and interesting guides, just whiling away time waiting until a stray tourist stumbles upon their beloved piece of history and they can spring into cheery 'information' mode. Occasionally a spider-fly-sticky web scenario flits across my brain, but rarely. Even if that is the case, I hope I thanked them all adequately for their infectious enthusiasm. Of my conversation with the cheery Cape Otway guide, I didn't think to ask him an obvious question: "What's the difference between a lighthouse and a lightstation?" Regrettably, the answer to that is still pending.

The next stretch of the coast is known as Shipwreck Coast and not without good reason. You can see rusting anchors and various bits of various wrecks at various points. Sadly, the road runs a little bit back from the coast, so short excursions are needed to see the points of interest – such as Moonlight Head, the Twelve Apostles (limestone stacks in the sea), London Bridge with one fallen arch, The Arch and Loch Ard Gorge, named after the wrecked Loch Ard from which only one crew member and one non-swimmer passenger survived: both aged 18.

Undeterred by the necessary excursions, I continued my zigzag route ticking off the tourist spots in true tourist fashion.

Unsurprisingly, I kept bumping into the same people as we all shuttled from one scenic spot to the next. Board walks mark the paths from the car parks to the viewpoints to preserve the land, but they don't add to the beauty of the area and they act as a reminder that on this stretch... at least... you are never alone. By the time I had reached this part of the Great Ocean Road a sea fret was rolling in which resulted in grey blurry photographs of what should have been dramatic scenery; that's where postcards come in handy.

As ever, time was not on my side so I nodded briefly at Port Campbell, Peterborough and Warrnambool, where the whale watching scenario had certainly been too optimistic, and continued westwards before arriving at five-thirty, exhausted, in Port Fairy, an ex-whaling station, 'Where the Past is Present'. The first thing that struck me was the really wide streets – of course, wide enough to turn an ox cart in. The first hotel I spotted was full, so by default found myself at the Seacombe House Motor Inn which, like Port Fairy itself 'is steeped in history' relating, I guess, to whalers, sailors and shipwrecks. The old part of the property dates back to 1847 and I stayed in Gun Alley, where, in hindsight, the three windows I marked on my memorabilia brochure look rather less romantic than the name implies. Happily the room was very comfortable and the melting moment with a cup of tea, both of which vanished rather rapidly, were very welcome after a long day on the road.

Dined in their *Good Food* recommended restaurant and sampled the fish, assuming that it would have come straight from the ocean over which I had been gazing. Not sure that my fish had swum in the Southern Ocean, or if it had, it hadn't done so recently. Happy to report, no harm done. I'm not a fussy eater, but am weirdly consistent in my dud choices, which I then feel compelled to write about. Not only does eating alone over an extended period, elevate the norm into something of note, there is also the tendency to greedily bolt food when companionless. A book or something to read slows down the process and stops you having to stare into space whilst munching and ruminating over the day's activities. The only problem with a book, especially a paperback, is that the open pages have a habit of binging closed just as you have a forkful of food a smidge away from your salivating mouth. Stupidly, instinct deems the book more important than the food so you drop the laden fork as you try to hang-on to the page you are reading. Consequently, food and fork complete a perfect arc before splattering back onto the table. You then scoop up the debris whilst taking a surreptitious peek at your fellow diners... wondering if they have witnessed your pantomime. Well, that's what happened at the Seacombe House Motor Inn... where my book of choice was a Dickensian tome, *Dombey and Son*, selected from my OU stash.

Returning to my delightfully chintzy room, the day ended with a feeling of self-satisfaction, I had notched up all but two of the places on my day's agenda. Spurred on by this success, I planned tomorrow's excursions cosily tucked up in bed... although I did remain a tiny bit alert in case the famed ghost of Thomas McCracken put in an appearance. He didn't. Unfortunately said Mr McCracken died from a cracked skull sustained in an alcohol fuelled altercation... *should I believe everything I read?*

Saturday 13th April: did I really think I was going to manage all of the following, plus yesterday's unseen Mount Gambier?

Having been drawn by chance to a brochure extolling the beauty of the Limestone Coast, I couldn't resist. So Portland was scratched from yesterday's incomplete itinerary and another twelve destinations took its place – they were:

- Beachport, an unspoilt haven and ex-whaling station
- Robe, an old fishing settlement and port
- Hindmarsh Island to see the mouth of the mighty Murray River
- Port Eliot on the prettily named Fleurieu Peninsula
- Victor Harbor, famed for a spelling mistake amid its seafaring past
- Waitpinga Beach, with a tiny population swelled by intrepid surfers… a stretch of coast not for the novice
- Cape Jervis and its port used by the Kangaroo Island Ferry
- Port Noarlunga for an 800m snorkel trail
- Strathalbyn, a Scottish heritage town
- Hahndorf, the oldest German settlement
- Tailem Bend, a strategic railhead
- And the Murray Bridge.

So how did I do? Breakfast was a scrum, thanks to a large golf contingent and one harassed waitress, so just grabbed a bowl of cereal before stepping outside to wander around Port Fairy, in the drizzle. It is such a pretty town, but I had no time to do it justice as I wanted to go inland to take a look at Mount Gambier. Stashing George, I pointed the Lancer in the hoped for right direction (north) and set off once again. The route was in contrast to what I had driven before. I passed miles and miles of grassland, bleached blond by the relentless summer sun, so cattle and sheep were grazing on grass frazzled to hay. More warnings to look out for wandering kangaroos and koalas… so far have only seen one dead of each; it would be nice to see one that's still breathing.

At the Mount Gambier information office picked up some maps and leaflets and headed to the extinct volcano's largest crater, which was impressive due to its text-book symmetry… it appeared in nature just as one would draw a crater… if that makes sense. The crater-lake is enticingly named the Blue

Lake, as it takes on a startling shade of blue under the right conditions. Predictably these conditions were not prevailing on the day of my visit, as the rain-laden sky had produced water that was a familiar English Channel shade of grey. I read that from November the water changes from 'steel blue-grey' to 'brilliant turquoise blue', so I guess it had peaked and was now reverting to the grey end of the spectrum. Irrespective of its colour, the leaflet informed me that a staggering '3,500 million litres of water is extracted each year for residential, commercial and industrial use', including the production of hand-made Blue Lake paper.

If I had been a little disappointed by Mount Gambier's lack of blueness, my visit did at least provide me with the answer to an avian puzzle. In the morning, I had been awoken by and intrigued by a loud, possibly indescribable, bird call and here were half a dozen of the species gabbling away in front of me. Their plumage made their genus obvious... they were Australian magpies. They made a human vowel sound – a-eee-i-ooo, which tailed off into a can't really be bothered attempt at u. Best I can do...

Back in the car I drove through a stretch of boring landscape, which was unusual as nothing before today had struck me as boring, until I hit the Limestone Coast. Wow! The brochure hadn't lied. And why hadn't anyone told me about this area before I set off? I would have added even more days to my already extended stay. With regret I had no time to explore properly, but (again) vowed I would return one day. Along this stretch, the sea which gently washes the beaches is a delicate shade of turquoise thanks to the limestone (no English Channel grey here!) The coast is riddled with caves and blow holes, but sadly no time to investigate: poor planning.

However, stopped at Beachport, an historic whaling port, for lunch and found the place deserted, as everyone was at Robe for the tall ships and little ships racing. Beachport's claim to fame is its jetty which, at 772 metres, is the second longest in

South Australia. I think the longest is virtually double the length and is located at Port Germein. It's funny, but each town or area seems to promote its uniqueness by having the largest, longest, highest... whatever. Possibly in such a very large country, if you're very small people pass you by, so promoting the biggest thing you have makes touristic sense. Anyway, the extent of the shallow water necessitated the construction of these long jetties, as ships couldn't get close to the shore. Today the ships have been replaced by anglers who, lured towards a sunny spot, dangle their lines in the hope of hauling in something fit for the table. Beachport sits on Rivoli Bay famed for its crayfish, and a fishing fleet still goes in search of these tasty crustaceans. *Why weren't they on last night's menu?*

When I arrived at Robe it was, unsurprisingly, very crowded but, finding a spot to park, I managed to worm my way up to a vantage point to look at the tall ships, just tiny dots in the distance, but one of which was going like the clappers – truly a ship at full sail. I think it was Russian. The town also hosts a major South Australian surf contest. Along the Limestone Coast you really feel the pull of the sea; it is a beautiful area and I was surprised that I had not heard about it before – but how lucky to stumble upon it. Serendipity, a delight of tumbleweed travels... you never know what lies up ahead.

Having made a few enquiries soon discovered that there was no accommodation in Robe because of the weekend activities, so pushed on to Kingston which is home to Larry the Lobster – all 33 metres of him. It was quite difficult trying to fit him into a camera shot without making him appear more small shrimp rather than large lobster. See, another 'large' attraction. I now know that Kingston is also home to one of few analematic sundials in the world which is a horizontal sundial marking solar time. Oh dear! One really should read the more obscure guide books before striking out, because there are some fascinating gems hidden just under the main tourist radar, and I had missed this one. Alas a lesson learnt a little too late. And Serendipity can be a fickle travel companion.

Although Kingston wasn't on my schedule, checked into a Best Western for a night on the beach, earlier than usual as the next bed would have been approximately two hours away and there are only so many miles I can drive in a day. Driving is helped along by alliterative slogans, such as 'Drowsy Drivers Die' or perhaps 'Drink, Drive, Die in a Ditch', plus assorted short poems urging caution. The black markers beside the road recall where a death has occurred and the red version marks where accidents have happened. These plus all the 'Kangaroos for the next 12km' signs set at every 13km, result in a lot to read, keeping you thoughtfully occupied with, umm, your eyes off the road...

Larry the Lobster... another large attraction...

Sitting in the bar with my usual tipple of cold beer and studying my newly acquired maps, I realised that I couldn't do all that I had intended in the time available, something had to go. Reluctantly I deleted the Fleurieu Peninsula, with its southerly tip Cape Jervis, from my itinerary to head north towards Tailem Bend and onwards to the Barossa Valley. By now my glass had emptied as had the bar...and somehow it was an eerily quiet 11pm.

Sunday 14th April: a slightly less ambitious itinerary today

Birdwood for a vintage car collection and the Barossa Valley
for vineyards

Haven't quite got distances and times sorted out – today's
plan went a bit awry. Interesting chat with a couple from
Coonawarra at breakfast, they were most concerned that I was
driving alone and told me not to stop for any bandaged person
waving me down, as it was a ruse to get me to stop. The blood
was tomato sauce and an accomplice would leap from the hedge
and beat me up. So, with that cheery thought buzzing in my
head, took a quick stroll along the beach and then set off for
Meningie, the railway town of Tailem Bend and the Murray
Bridge, the first bridge over the Murray. A really relaxing drive,
with long stretches of not a lot but still beguiling. Stopped at
a pelican viewing point on Lake Albert, but sadly no pelicans;
am beginning to think someone forewarns the wildlife of my
imminent arrival. Had lunch, a real one this time, of a ham
ploughman's and a lite beer in the German town of Hahndorf.

Hahndorf was settled by the Germans in 1840 and my idea
had been to look at the old stone cottages, but they were plastered
over with signs proclaiming 'Devon Cream Teas', 'Bratwurst and
chips' and it was heaving with people like me: tourists. Anyway,
enjoyed my lunch and then headed off towards the Barossa
Valley via Birdwood where I stumbled across an incredible treat;
the National Motor Museum. My timing for once was spot on
as the museum was holding a 1970s themed exhibition with a
sporty lime green Holden taking centre stage, alongside the last
Mini to come off the Australian production line plus photos and
clothes from the era and a macramé owl… *Why were they ever
popular?*

Vehicles from the earliest that bounced over Australia's
unmetalled roads to the latest beasts of burden, the mighty
trucks used to haul road trains across the outback, were lined up

in all their mechanical glory. Gazing up at the road truck's lofty cab, I was unaware that one day I would discover just how much dust these machines throw up in passing. This was an evocative and engaging collection which really captured my imagination. It's always hard to know exactly what stamps an enduring impression on your brain, but this museum will remain firmly etched in my memory for years to come, of that I am sure.

Earlier in the day the brilliant sunshine had disappeared behind a curtain of heavy cloud but as I emerged from the museum, I was greeted by a bright blue sky. The sun lit up the colours of the trees, tucked in amongst softly rounded hills passed which I drove, drinking in the sheer beauty of my surroundings. I ventured up the Lofty Range to Angaston, the highest point in the Barossa Valley and home to the Yalumba vineyards and then on to Nuriootpa, where the Wolf Bass vineyards are to be found. I had naïvely hoped to find somewhere cheap and cheerful to stay in this centre of viticulture, but with night-time approaching the only hotel was the Novotel Resort nestled in a prime spot. Gazing across the view that guests would surely enjoy with a glass or two of the Barossa's finest, I decided that the price-tag would be as prime as the setting. With a sigh, I regretted that this luxury was not for me and flipped a mental coin in lieu of spinning a compass. Ruminations over, and as the early evening was so peaceful, opted to drive down towards Adelaide.

Slight snag though, in those pre-android days, no film left in my camera and nowhere to buy one. A tunnel of gum trees, oh so photogenic, opened up at Jacobs Creek, especially noted for the Shiraz vines, acres of them. Drove across the creek itself which was little more than a trickle at that time of year, and also doffed my cap at Penfolds. Still nowhere to rest my now increasingly weary head, got careless at a crossroads when turning right; luckily the road was empty but it gave my search a more urgent edge... but to no avail. Won't bore you with details of the increasing number of detours I took trying to find a bed, but on the edge of Adelaide I found a good old Best Western, a chain which is rapidly replacing Travelodge in my affections. I spent the night slobbed in front of Julia Roberts and Susan Sarandon, in the syrupy *Stepmom* which was just the tonic after a long day!

... A photogenic tunnel of gum trees... no film in my camera...

So having travelled north and back, I am now in the suburbs of Adelaide, the 'City of Churches' or the home of the Hills hoist, aka the garden twirly whirly on which to hang your washing. Tomorrow I might just as well head south to the Fleurieu Peninsula after all. Oh, I wish I could describe today's drive in a way that would really do it justice. The Limestone Coast section was incredible, admittedly it was uber flat, but that just increased the beauty of the open skies. Driving in these conditions created a weird sensation. At one point mackerel clouds washed across the blue sky but the sun filtering through them was painfully bright. To prevent wrinkle-inducing squinting, I put on my sunglasses and the clouds which I had been driving towards, suddenly seemed to turn and rush towards me, which was a tad alarming. So, I took off my glasses, the clouds retreated and I carried on squinting. I have since learnt that my eyes don't like brown-tinted sunglasses, which is a rather bizarre.

Back to the TV and suddenly *Stepmom* has become less of a tonic and more of an irritation – it's lasting forever thanks to adverts every ten minutes; this is truly testing my dedication to viewing. Will multi-task, watch TV and continue to pen the odd thought related to my Great Ocean Road experience...

I took as long (or short) as the standard Trailfinders information seemed to indicate appropriate, I think I added one day, but on reflection this was far too short a stretch of time. I wanted to explore more beaches along the way, and spend longer at those that I did visit. I really wish I had taken more photographs and I must have been off my trolley to drive through the Barossa Valley without a film in my camera. Perhaps you stop thinking logically when you are on your own. I might nag a partner about "Have you got... *blahbiddyblah*..." but am unlikely to nag myself. Also, at the beginning of this jaunt I really should have allocated an entire day to Ballarat as I severely underestimated how much there was to see and do in the area. Had I spent the first night in Ballarat and then headed off after breakfast, that following day would have marked day one of the Great Ocean Road journey.

Doing it my way, it was getting late and the light was fading by the time I reached Cape Otway and the point where the scenery was becoming really interesting. Plus I added the Limestone Coast. Irrespective of any tweaking that could have been done, all in all it was an amazing experience: *thank you very much.*

Monday 15th April: down to the coast at Cape Jervis

Pottered in the morning – aided by the fact that I had toast and cereal facilities in my room, but by ten decided that I really ought to get going. With some reluctance, I vacated my room for another stint behind the wheel of my car, the reluctance probably due to the impending end of my freewheeling adventure and not the thought of racking up more miles. When asked in later years if I ever got lonely on my travels, my eyeballs would react in a pop-eyed questioning 'why?' way. I had George with me. Admittedly with each re-emergence from car boot or plane hold he looked a little more battle weary, but he proved to be the perfect guardian of my goods and chattels. And as an added bonus, his one squeaky wheel acted as an effective warning siren clearing our passage as, in tandem, we breezed through yet another air terminal or trundled up to another hotel reception desk. A more dependable travelling companion a girl could not wish for.

That said, back to today... when I was mildly surprised at how full the hotel car park was as I steered said companion, the increasingly independently minded George, between rows of parked cars fearful of scratching polished paintwork. As I wasn't one hundred per cent sure where to go for the day, we set off towards Port Adelaide and then spotting signs to Cape Jervis, changed my mind and headed that way instead. It's that sort of impromptu manoeuvre which adds to the fun of solo travel – explanations or excuses are not needed. More vineyards in the McLaren Vale area and once again, beautiful scenery down from the Adelaide Hills and across a flat plain and up again into the hills which run down to the Cape. Very twisty road with lots of red and black markers to keep me focused, or perhaps distracted, drove through avenues of majestic gums... still without a film in my camera. *Couldn't I have bought one from or near the hotel...?*

Arrived at Cape Jervis in the blistering heat and bought a cold drink and, I am truly ashamed, a hot doughnut from a caravan parked in the car park by the tiny quay: calorific perfection. There was very little to see down by the harbour, except for the looming bulk of the Kangaroo Island Ferry, which was waiting for the off. Licking jam from my fingers, I drove back up the hill into the village and finally managed to track down some film and then returned to take photos of the departing ferry. As time was doing its usual trick, retraced my steps and decided to detour to Port Noarlunga, which is 34km south of Adelaide. It's a picturesque beachside town where I had lunch and wrote some postcards and then realised that I would have to head back to Adelaide as the Lancer was due to be dropped off that evening.

My internal navigation system reckoned that if I just kept going, I ought to arrive in the area of West Terrace which would then require a right turn into North Terrace, easy, the home of Avis. Indeed, I did make it to North Terrace with relative ease and then spent a certain amount of time cruising up and down, with buses and taxis in close proximity, until finally in amongst the tree-lined avenue I spotted the tiny Avis sign I was looking for. After an exhilarating 1690km (1050 miles) I was sad to part with another hire car, but at least all was okay. Still think the odometers are not recording all that I've driven…

The hotel was a two-minute walk away and tired but happy, I checked in. H'mm, just what is the time I thought to ask. My watch was showing five and the hotel clock four. Having put my watch forward by thirty minutes on crossing into South Australia at Mount Gambier that was the time I had assumed for the last few days. In making the adjustment, what I hadn't appreciated was the fact that South Australia had remained on 'regular time' whilst Eastern Australia had changed onto daylight saving. Therefore the half an hour forward, should in fact have been half an hour back… which explains things like empty restaurants in the evenings and full car parks in the mornings; I was an hour out. It also explained why the barman at the hotel in Kingston looked a little bemused when I determinedly claimed my 'free beer' at four in the afternoon. A thirty-minute time difference between two adjacent time zones, plus the added complication of inconsistently applied daylight saving does seem confusing… about as confusing as my explanation.

But the bonus came when after a bath and relax it was still daylight and I had time to explore the pretty city of Adelaide. The city had a hard act to follow – Melbourne had really won my heart. The central part of Adelaide, the old city, is surprisingly small and therefore walkable, which is just as well, as there is only one tram in the city and it runs out to Glenelg on the coast. Sadly, there was no time to explore that route. From my email home:

> … if you're still hanging on in there, you now find me in Adelaide after a 1,600km drive which began in Melbourne and carried me through diverse scenery of coast and hills, forest and vineyards. I have met some fascinating characters and now realise that gum trees come in more than one variety, from small gnarled versions to great soaring sentinels and, borrowing a word from Dame Edna, some truly spooky versions. Again, my camera is struggling to do Australia justice. It's a bit alarming seeing so many signs warning me of koalas and roos and I guess they mean the live variety rather than the few I have seen lying on their backs with their paws in the air. Also saw pelicans again, not where expected, but bobbing about in various bits of coastal waters, also heard strange noises in the bush… butcher birds perhaps.
>
> Melbourne was fascinating and I managed to cram in a goodly amount of sightseeing in two days. Am now in the home of the Barossa Valley and Adelaide Hills wines and enjoying a purely objective sampling spree…

Tuesday 16th April: a day of sightseeing

Began the day with an email session: faster and cheaper than New Zealand. Then went shopping, splashing out on two pairs of long trousers and a top. Not quite sure how I am going to squeeze everything into George, who, like his owner, is beginning to look a little bloated. The hotel provided me with a map of a three-hour walk which took in the main sights. Some attractive Victorian architecture remains, especially the old shopping arcade, plus one or two handsome examples of Art Nouveau. Took lots of photos but no time to visit Ayers (as in the rock) House, as self-guided tours not possible and regrettably had no time to wait for the official tour. From 1855–1897 the house had been the opulent home of Sir Henry Ayers, Premier of South Australia and it would have been lovely to take a peek inside. Sir Henry had made his fortune in the copper mining industry, so I guess he was able to accumulate some fine artefacts.

Banishing my disappointment, the Botanic Garden came to the rescue and reaffirmed my view that Australia is home to some immaculate and diverse public gardens. I wandered amongst an array of weird and wonderful plants including a 'lost world' collection of primeval cycads. There seemed to be many more palms outside the Palm House than in it, and everything was in tip top condition. Having missed his house, I discovered that Sir Henry had been a governor of the gardens: a delightful legacy for the citizens of Adelaide and much enjoyed by me.

Ended the day in the Art Gallery of South Australia and that was an absolute and unexpected treat. The paintings were displayed beautifully, with a wide range of European and North American works from the Renaissance to modern art. For me, however, the stars of the collection were the Australian and Australian Aboriginal works. I'm not sure how long I stood before Tom Roberts' atmospheric 1891 painting entitled *A break away!*

It depicts a drover on horseback trying to deflect stampeding, thirst-crazed sheep from careering destructively headlong towards a dam. The dust and drama portrayed in the painting has come to epitomise the grit of the pioneering pastoralists. After the drama of life in the outback, a change in tempo was to be had browsing the exquisite displays of furniture, glass, silver and a host of marble and bronze statues. A Roman torso, *The Bowmore Artemis*, was another stellar artefact. I wanted to ruffle the billowy folds of her gathered tunic, but the huntress would have broken my fingers, she was sculpted from marble. Full marks: the art gallery is a sparkling jewel in Adelaide's crown.

It was in the gallery that I decided it was hard to refute the adage that 'travel broadens the mind'. At some time in the future I would have to come up with a research topic for a masters degree (hence the excess book baggage). Looking at the work of contemporary indigenous artists, I saw how they, through their creativity, were connecting with and reclaiming their past. I was looking at pictorial representations of an oral creation narrative, in particular the representations of Dreamtime. Without that *eureka* moment in Adelaide, I might never have argued, through *Honey Ant Dreaming*, that the ancient oral narratives of the Australian Aboriginal Dreamtime have a contemporary relevance. Through the resilience of narratives, passed down through the generations, they have helped a dispossessed society to reclaim its cultural heritage. Sitting at my desk in England, my research took me back to my son's adopted country and its ancient history. *Thank you*, Adelaide.

At the beginning of this book, I exhorted 'empty nesters' to go off and have an adventure… and I reiterate that view… go and grab a few more rocking chair moments just as our children are doing. Perhaps not necessarily tie it in with further studies as, I concede, how the dickens do you study Dickens when driving around Oz? And yes, *Dombey and Son* is a bit of a leap away from *Honey Ant Dreaming* … but it's all about stepping stones.

Sydney and Canberra: from Blue to Snowy Mountains

Wednesday 17th April: last few hours in Adelaide and then back to Sydney

Another quick email then off to collect some photos of the Great Ocean Road which had been developed overnight. Thumbing through the prints, sadly the results proved to be no better, in fact worse, than the average one-hour service, plus two of the photos were scratched. Can't blame the developers for the subject matter – can't believe how much I hadn't photographed and I still seem to be mastering the camera judging by the amount of black shadow. Oh well, back-up postcards are obviously the way forward.

Next on the list was the South Australia Museum, where I started in the dinosaur exhibition which, unsurprisingly, was teeming with small children as this was the autumn break. Moved on to the rest of the museum where the highlights proved to be the superb displays of South Sea Islands' artefacts plus the mineral collection, although here the labelling seemed a bit erratic. For me to spend ages looking at lumps of rock was something totally novel – *possibly the Wai-O-Tapu effect*?

Returned to the hotel with time for a quick Cascade Lite

beer and then clambered aboard the airport bus, ready for the next leg of my journey. Gazing from the window, bidding a silent farewell to Adelaide, I spotted two gentlemen deep in conversation, one sporting an ill-disguised toupee and the other clutching a carrier bag from the stationers, Wigg & Co... If life sometimes gets you down, it's equally capable of producing moments of unexpected 'laugh out loud' humour. Not that I was particularly down, but I did let out a tiny hiccup-like squeak.

George and I experienced another straightforward flight, and in a little under two hours our bumpy landing announced our arrival back in Sydney, and the first rain for several days. Took the train into town and liaised with Matt to meet for a drink at the Stanley Hotel (really a pub, but termed 'hotel' because of the pokies). Hauled George from the station platform, lugged him up a flight of steps, and as I emerged at street level, fell *splat* onto the pavement. Homebound workers just stepped around me, seemingly convinced that I was something of a drunken bag lady. One of the first rules of solo travel: you must be able to lift and carry your own baggage without either popping your vertebrae or falling flat on your face or both.

Soberly, I gathered myself up, inspected my knees, and tottered off to find the rendezvous point where I settled into a corner, an unloved George hidden under the table. With a schooner of the now familiar, coolly welcoming non-Lite version of Cascade in my grasp, my spirits were restored. Alice was the first to find me, quickly followed by Matt; another beer and then off for a bowl of pasta back at Yurong Street. Joy of joys, it was like coming home.

Thursday 18th April: a theatrical experience

I awoke to a washing and shopping morning, steering clear of any controversial domestic cleaning. Enjoyed a wander around Sydney where I behaved like a small child thumping the pedestrian buttons on the traffic lights. The sound they make to alert visually impaired people that it's safe to cross, is just... well... so Sydney and I can't reproduce it on paper. And of course, I only thumped the buttons when I actually wanted to cross the roads...

Met Matt in Darling Harbour in the afternoon and then joined Alice and their friend John for a drink prior to a Kung Fu night with the Shaolin Monks, at the Gothic, Italian, Art Deco confection that is the listed State Theatre. Its designer had obviously seen Orsanmichele in Florence as an exact replica of Donatello's *St George* stands to attention in the entrance to the foyer. Just a thought, the theatre stands on Market Street close to its intersection with George Street... could that have anything to do with the choice of saint?

Excellent evening of sweaty exploits in sumptuous surroundings, signed off with a pizza supper and then bed. I've loved my travels, but I feel so at home in Sydney.

Friday 19th April: the Blue Mountains

The day began with another tasty egg-fest breakfast this time not beside the sea, but in a tiny café next to Paddington, one of the more colourful areas of Sydney. In a hired car, we then drove out of town to the Blue Mountains. Not sure what I was expecting, or why I felt so over-awed, but the mountain range is magnificent. At our first stopping spot, a densely tree-clad vista stretched ahead for miles and miles whilst to one side there stood the famous kilometre high (above sea level) peaks, known as the Three Sisters. So closely packed do the trees appear, that it seems impossible for hikers to follow the trails and squeeze a way through. The distant blue wash hanging in the air comes from the haze created by the eucalyptus oil which rises from the trees turning the air blue... in a good way.

Next we parked at Katoomba and walked along a tiny track with red tailed black cockatoos, bush turkeys and assorted other birds for company. Dog-trotted past streams, waterfalls, ferns, mosses, ironwood trees and gums galore; Matt and Alice can yomp at quite a pace. Not wishing to let my son down, uncomplainingly I also yomped along, bringing up the rear, getting red of face and short of wind, pretending that I 'up hill and down dale' on a daily basis. My diet was obviously not helping my stamina. I learnt that touching the wood of an ironwood tree is reputed to make you barren; happily three daughters later this old wives tale was disproved by Alice.

Having descended into the Jamison Valley via a series of steep steps, we thankfully *phew* ascended swiftly courtesy of a 'scenic rider' which whooshed us up to the top, in no time at all. You feel as if you're sitting in a rusty bucket as you're hauled aloft over a distance of over 300 metres with an incline of 52 degrees; an incline which seemingly translates into the perpendicular. Sadly everything changes and I think that since 2013 the exhilarating 'rider' has become more sophisticated without a hint of the characterful rust anywhere. Progress! After that little adrenalin buzz, we made our way back to the car via another spectacular uppy, downy walking route – and I certainly felt the result of all this exercise the next morning! My calf muscles were bleating pitifully.

It was a 100km drive back to Sydney, giving us enough time for a quick wash and brush-up then off to have dinner with John (our theatre-going companion). For his assembled guests, he created a Jamie Oliver inspired meal with plenty of booze. I have a hazy recollection of excellent food, excellent company and finding my bed just a little before daybreak.

Thought for the day: everyone is so welcoming. Sydney is renowned as being a 'young persons' city, but in reality the

Sydney-siders don't seem at all age conscious. Here I was having the most wonderful time and realising that I could never say to Matt, "Come Home". This was home. I have no regrets about smashing the cross-eyed apprehensive piggy bank to investigate his new surroundings: mission accomplished!

Saturday 20th April: from Blue to Snowy Mountains

Matt and Alice spent the morning flat-hunting and found an ideal place in Birchgrove with an impressive view of Sydney and the harbour. I stayed at the house and pottered prior to our trip to the Snowy Mountains. Having struck lucky and found a flat, there followed a fair amount of scrabbling around to get the paperwork sorted out before putting in their offer. The idea was to deliver the necessary bits and pieces before setting off on our journey. By happy coincidence, the flat was above the estate agent's office, so having pushed the papers under the door of the (by now) closed office, we sat and admired the external elevation of the flat, which was accessed via a very twisty spiral staircase.

Alice hadn't seen inside the flat as it was the last viewing of the morning and despondency had set in but she bravely trusted Matt's judgement and was in favour of applying. As good luck would have it, the current tenant appeared and then proceeded to give them both a guided tour. Matt was surprised that he had misremembered some of the layout and Alice wasn't overawed by the high ceilings. However, when compared to the competition viewed previously, it received a resounding thumbs-up. So with all done that could be done our attention was drawn to assorted hunger pangs, which were finally sated by plates of baked beans and Marmite. Vegemite has failed to usurp its English counterpart on my family's palate, which means that each and every time I arrive in Australia I have to stand in line to declare my numerous pots of salty black condiment to a bored-looking customs official.

And then – finally – we were off, heading southwest and into heavy rain. A dramatic five-hour journey ensued with a tiny bit of white-knuckle (mine) aquaplaning. A petrol stop at Goulburn allowed me to add another big 'thing' to my Larry the Lobster list. This time it was the Big Merino aka Rambo – wish I had been able to take a photo but at least he (along with all the other whacky big art) appears on several internet sites.

At last we reached Thredbo and what a fabulous spot… even in the pouring rain and pitch dark I knew this was somewhere special. We stayed in a delightful cabin beside the Thredbo River, where my bed was up a steep ladder in the loft whilst my hosts had a pretty double room downstairs. I loved my lofty space from where I could peer over the balcony down into the living area and retrieve mugs of tea or coffee which appeared from time to time at the top of my ladder. It was all so very, very lovely. Alice was determined to cook on our arrival so as soon as she had extricated herself from the car was to be heard biffing and banging away in the kitchen. In less than twenty minutes we were tucking into hot pasta bathed in tuna and tomato sauce – my contribution was to tidy the kitchen afterwards. Just as well I was doing something, as my carb intake was still on the up – *you'll note muffins have given way to pasta…*

Climbing back up my ladder to sleep, I was suddenly transported back to childhood when I had read the Heidi books written by Johanna Spyri. I had yearned to live in a wooden hut on the mountain, listening to cow bells gently announcing the whereabouts of their wearers, rather than in suburban Wandsworth listening to the thrum of passing cars. With the predictable unpredictability of my brain digging up something I would have thought long forgotten, I drifted off to sleep dreaming of goats' cheese, flower-strewn green grass, cow bells and alpine vistas.

Sunday 21st April: on top of the world

Unsurprisingly, I slept soundly in my elevated dream-inducing bed and awoke to be greeted by a grey and cloudy day which could not mar the glorious view of the stream running below our verandah and upon which waddled two plump ducks. Fortified by raisin toast for breakfast we set off for mount Kosciuszko with rations of Kojak lollies and bananas as substitutes for Kendal mint cake.

A chair lift takes you to a point at the beginning of a twelve kilometre walk to the mountain's summit. This is the area over which Matt and Alice ski in the winter, so it's always fun to know how many boulders and bumps you are skiing over. The weather was still far from ideal as cloud and mist were rolling around obscuring the view and a biting wind was blowing. Undeterred, we strode out along a metal walkway, strategically placed to prevent further erosion, with lollies firmly gripped between teeth which otherwise would have started their own chilly chattering. I was very pleased with my New Zealand decision to invest in a pair of thick trousers as they worked well at keeping the lower part of me warm, and they *weren't* too long. Warmth to the top half was provided by an extremely attractive beige waterproof jacket bought especially for New Zealand but which, for some reason, had remained unworn. It's the sort of garment that comes into its own in inclement weather, but if the weather stays fine, you end up wondering why you both bought and brought it.

So, yes it was cold and blowy but the conditions created a magical, mystical experience. Clouds scurried and whirled across the sky, parting every once in a while to reveal tantalising distant glimpses of the Snowy Mountains – a bit Philip Pullman and his *Dark Materials* trilogy... you really did feel there was another world behind that slit in the clouds. At some point the walkway vanished and we were meandering by babbling brooks, small ponds, lichens and mosses all of which had created their own small worlds within this dramatic, boulder-strewn lunar landscape. But it was very, very windy especially so when crossing gullies down which the wind whistled so hard that it invited you to stop and play... arms outstretched, legs splayed seeing if the wind would tip you from your feet and send you airborne over the scraggy terrain. It didn't, but it seemed only a puff away from success.

Onwards and upwards we climbed until the summit was reached where, Alice, glancing skywards proclaimed, in the words of her granny, that there was "enough blue to make a pair of pants for a sailor". Only for those tailors swift enough with the cutting shears as the blue kept rapidly disappearing and reappearing until it finally vanished for good. Still, the blowy sense of achievement at having reached our destination was rewarded with an ice-cold solid banana. Alice is a whizz at producing some necessary and appreciated nourishment just at the right sugar-ebbing moment.

Having arrived at the top and grinned, or blue-faced grimaced, through the necessary moment-capturing photo-shoot, down we headed to the point where the wind whistles with maximum gusto from all directions and there, also hanging on for dear life, were two handily placed portaloos: how civilised! If someone had taken the trouble to cart them up there, the least I could do was to utilise the facilities. Soap, mirror and all mod cons plus a feeling that I had stepped into Dr Who's Tardis... with the wind howling under the door and gently rocking the bright blue cabin perhaps a bit of time-travel was imminent? I'm not sure that I've ever stumbled across strategically placed portaloos during country-side rambles in England, or if I have, I've never had the nerve to use them. Here it just seems natural to find them 'out of the blue'.

Continuing the descent, we reached the top of the chairlift and faced decision time – to take the easy (if wobbly) aerial route or the energetic land-hike down to the valley? No decision really. The downward trek, unlike the ascent, followed a vague path which wove backwards and forwards under the chairlift. "Did you fall off?" a pair of dangling boots seemed to ask.

Slithering southwards, I was convinced I was about to slip in an unladylike fashion on the long wet grass, which had now replaced the boulders. Deciding to save face (or bottom), I adopted a weird crab-like motion and successfully, if not attractively, mastered the descent in a reasonably independent fashion. There was only one "help me" moment when my feet argued about which way to go, so I ended up with one foot pointing at three o'clock and its partner at nine o'clock whilst my body tipped forward in a favoured noon position. A helping hand sorted me out. All this drama did not detract our attention from the intoxicating whiffs which assailed our nostrils: tea tree, we thought. Plus we were kicking up lots of animal spore of assorted shapes and sizes: wombats and brumbies – the feral horses, descendents of an earlier pioneering chapter in Australia's history. The more I learn about this country, the more there is to learn... a cliché perhaps, but an honest one.

Back in Thredbo, refreshed by lunch of a soft drink and peanut bar, we pottered around the shops and generally drifted close to the House of Ullr waiting for the bar to open. At last, a much-needed beer and a challenging game of darts. The barman had been in the valley since 1987, drawn by the skiing. He spoke of the spring flowers which few people saw as no one travelled in the period leading up to Christmas. (Journal note: perhaps an option with husband in tow one year...) Alice, a self-proclaimed darts novice proved to be an ace at circles... or was it cricket... either way it was a dart variant that I have now forgotten how to play. And she was very good. Matt won at 501.

Our noisy laughter attracted Stephen, a local, who joined us for a game and upon the production of his personal set of tungsten darts, our laughter subsided: this was business.

Having spent the first half of 501 throwing darts anywhere and everywhere, except onto the board, managed to finish swiftly and niftily behind Matt throwing a double two and a one with two darts. Why, if I can do that, am I usually dart-throwing rubbish? We won! And Stephen wasn't the match we feared he might be. Warmed by the convivial beer and darts we wandered off in search of a bottle shop which just happened to be in a bar with a pool table. Unable to resist, Matt and Alice played with the help of two small boys who lodged themselves firmly at the sides of the table, if not under the armpits of the players, giving helpful hints and keeping their fingers crossed during difficult shots.

Game over, a small panic followed when my son realised that his jacket, complete with keys, money, etc., was nowhere to be found. Retracing our steps led us back to the Ullr bar where the barman, looking at his watch, said, "Well, what took you so long?" as he handed over said jacket, with precious contents all present and correct. Matt does have a history of absent-mindedly 'forgetting' things… although I'm still not certain as to the fate of his brand new cricket bat which went awol some eighteen years previously. Back at the cabin, we tucked into macaroni cheese, with bacon for the carnivores, and spinach salad. *Star Wars* took care of the rest of a truly special day.

A further word here about the proliferation of roadside bon mots, designed to act as public service notices ensuring a safe and healthy population. My growing collection now includes: 'Stop, revive, survive'; 'We like our lizards frilled not grilled'; 'The drain is only for the rain' (what else?) and 'Dozy drivers die' along with its 1950s schoolboy variant 'Be Alert… Australia needs lerts!' But Thredbo's contribution wins for puzzlement as it only makes sense when you know what it means (a bit like the drain message) 'when in the snow – the bin's the go', which refers to the use of personal butt bins for those nasty fag ends. Previously, when the ski season closed and the snows melted, the mountainside was littered with unappealing, soggy butts. Fascinating!

After all that exercise, it was back to our cabin for a mellow evening with a shared bottle of Australia's finest. Returning to a domestic routine is not going to be easy...

Monday 22nd April: hydro-electricity of my school days and Canberra

The day dawned rather brighter than Sunday, but we decided that as yesterday's walk had been perfect we wouldn't try to outdo its excellence with another and so, fortified by Danish and coffee, we set off for the Snowy Mountains Hydro Electric scheme and then Canberra. Once again, beautiful scenery – the Scottish Highlands with kangaroo warning signs. We arrived at the information centre and then watched a seventeen minute film about the scheme's conception and construction. My memories from school geography were sketchy. I had forgotten how large and numerous were the dams and also that during my school days, the site was still under construction – the work having commenced in 1950 was not completed until 1974. According to the publicity film it still copes well, however, the local press in Adelaide had described the friction between the farmers and the townies over the release of water: farms do well whilst the towns have to rely on the Murray River for their water and with falling levels they are facing dire shortages.

A trip out to one of the dams would have been great but as it needed a half day to fully gain from the experience, we had to opt out. Again, where are my photos? Sometimes I seem to have got so carried away admiring the scenery that I forgot to take any snaps and on other occasions I snapped away only to spend the evening wondering why I had been so repetitive and unimaginative in framing my shots. Oh well, I still seem to be on a long camera-learning curve.

Back in the car and onwards to Canberra… which came as a pleasant surprise. *What had I been expecting?* Admittedly it was a sunny day with the city's renowned trees adding a splash of colour in their autumnal garb. As expected there were many native eucalypts and river oaks, but unexpectedly there were deciduous trees from England, Roman cypress and probably specimens from other countries too. This wasn't a random approach to greening a created urban environment, careful planning had obviously gone into the planting schemes. Carriageways were separated by avenues of trees and shady arches were created from gracefully touching boughs. Damon had spoken of the 'tumbleweed' affect but the city seemed busy enough in a tiny bit *Witches of Eastwick* way: it was unnaturally pristine.

The grass roof of the Parliament building gave the impression that we had just stepped onto the set of *Teletubbies*. We managed a tour of Parliament House which as a building was modern and airy and as an institution, surprisingly interesting with the electorate sitting above the elected people's representatives – to remind the representatives of their duties and obligations towards those who voted them in, and who similarly have the power to vote them out. Lunch in the sun followed and then homeward bound via wooded hills and green valleys.

As a postscript to Canberra, if anyone had said in fourteen years' time you'll be cycling around Canberra's Lake Burley Griffin trying to keep up with your three granddaughters… I would have laughed. Such is life.

Back to now, and back in Sydney where the evening sustenance came in the form of pie and peas with mash and gravy at Harry's Café de Wheels, a Sydney 'pie and mash' institution that has been going since the depression years of the 1930s. Good honest food to stave off hunger pangs, it's not surprising that this concept of simple food dolled out from the window of a caravan has become an integral part of Sydney life.

Finished the day back in Yurong Street with a beer in bed! My beer calorie count must surely be exceeding the muffin tally? Just to set the record straight, I don't typically knock back the pints with such gusto back at home (and certainly not in bed) but beer does seem to be the fuel that's keeping me going. And of course, I'm committed to writing my journal… so a nightcap helps.

Beer and muffins – my staple diet

Tuesday 23rd April: a Sydney tourist and tears at *Rabbit-Proof Fence*

Awoke early and decided that as this was my penultimate day in Sydney, I would attend to housekeeping issues. Had shopping to do and films to be developed, was short of cash, wanted to buy a birthday present for Alice, clothes to be washed and car to return to Hertz. Managed the last two first and then by eleven o'clock was heading back through Hyde Park, passing by the none-too attractive scavenging straw-necked Ibis, in search of an ATM. Found one in a store and went through the keying-in process but *eek* no money came out. Thank heavens for the invention of mobile phones as phoned the helpline and was told that the debit had not registered so was able to find another machine (in a bank this time) and *hey presto* I was solvent again. Began searching for a suitable gift for Alice and finally decided upon a 'coffret' of L'Occitane soaps, oils, etc. and also bought Odette a perfumed candle. Not wishing to cart the gifts around, decided to retrace my steps back to the store later in the day.

Perhaps to know the nitty gritty of my shopping expedition does not make for compelling reading, but I think the sub-text relates to the way you can become suddenly fixated when travelling alone, even though staying with one's nearest and dearest. You decide to do something knowing time is not on your side and everything else just gets elbowed out of the way, until mission accomplished And it doesn't just relate to shopping, as I had an 'out of character' moment in Perth, but that comes later. And no, I didn't feel the urge to have a body tattoo… but I can now quite understand how it happens.

After that little digression, I headed down to the aquarium where I ate a cheese and ham croissant whilst fighting off marauding pigeons, before catching the ferry round to Circular Quay. On reflection, I should have conceded defeat and fed my lunch to the mangy birds as their need seemed greater than mine. The next ferry took me to Manly where I had a quick potter around and enjoyed a cup of coffee in the sunshine – unmolested by scavenging birds. On the beach by the ferry a sign warns bathers not to go in the harbour-side sea for twenty-four hours after rain due to the high levels of pollution the run-off creates, which is such a pity because it's a lovely spot with a real 1930s feel. Alice likens it to Brighton, but for me it has a less depressing air. For some reason, Brighton always seems to me to envelop itself in a wistful whiff of having seen better days (possibly due to the rust-inducing salty-weather battering it gets). Truly, I'm not going out of my way to offend the denizens of assorted towns… and I expect many towns only give up their secrets to those who bother to stay long enough to discover them.

A family from Malaysia befriended me on the trip to Manly – because I was carrying a small Kipling bag and their (adult) son carried a larger version. He and I were also jostling for prime photo opportunities... I so needed another shot of that rather splendid bridge. The family was very interested to hear that I was travelling alone and said that they were en route for Auckland where they would be staying for three days. I breezily said, "Don't be too surprised if it rains." Their crestfallen reaction signalled that this was a New Zealand concept they had not considered. Not sure how or why I managed to burst their sunny weather bubble. Just a bit of chatty conversation which backfired: I really hope they enjoyed three dry days and left NZ wondering what I had been talking about. It would have been a more productive trip if I had asked them to use my camera to photograph me, as, in those pre-selfie days, the human interest in all the wonderful sights I snapped was always the smiling faces of complete strangers.

After my brief visit to Manly, well only the Manly by the landing stage as there is still much more to see, I set off again on a ferry bound for Circular Quay and was entertained on the journey by the antics of a seagull balancing on the flagpole. As the boat rolled and swayed across the waves, he shifted his weight from one leg to two as he effortlessly maintained his balance. He kept up his balletic antics for a good twenty minutes, looking left and right at the views just as the passengers were doing, until he caught sight of a passing fishing boat and then was gone – off in search of his supper. The ferries were probably his preferred way of getting around the harbour.

Back on the wrong side of Darling Harbour, I again trudged over the Pyrmont Bridge and retraced my steps to collect another batch of mediocre photos plus the presents for Alice and Odette. I then wended my way back across Hyde Park keeping an eye open for a bottle-shop. Phoned Matt for advice who told me to turn through 180 degrees and walk two steps forwards and bingo bottle-shop, plus chemist to replenish my toothpaste supply and grocer's to replace their soft-rinse for the washing machine. Back to the house and the usual struggle with the keys at the outer gate and then a quick dash to get ready before walking back down to Circular Quay to meet my hosts at the cinema... (my legs worked hard that day and I guess I burnt off a few of those liquid calories).

Phoned to say that I was on my way as I was cutting it a bit fine, well, they hadn't told me about the venue or timing until I was having the bottle-shop conversation; finally arrived at the cinema, slightly warm, with two minutes to spare. Superb comfy cinema and the emotionally draining but not-to-be-missed *Rabbit-Proof Fence*: tears, tissues (my personal stash handed out to sobbing strangers up and down our row)... *boo hoo*.

The film was taken from the book written by Nugi Garimara, which describes events which led to Australia's lost generation of (usually) mixed race European-Aboriginal children being taken by force from their Aboriginal mothers. The story is Molly's story, Nugi's mother, who with her sister and cousin, Daisy and Gracie, escaped from the institution they had been taken to and walked the entire 1,600km home, across barren and remote tracts of Western Australia, avoiding police and Aboriginal trackers. The girls were aged eight, eleven and fourteen. Loud sobs echoed around the cinema

Bleary-eyed, teary-eyed, we held our usual pavement discussion about what to eat and where and finally settled on a pizza in The Rocks area which nestles in the shadow of the bridge, without the tiniest hint of its bubonic plague history. The location was handy as it gave me an idea of where I should head the following day. My choice of pumpkin pizza was as odd as it sounds and I doubt that I'll be in a hurry to have one again, but you have to try these things. A few beers led to a deep and meaningful family 'discussion' which happily no one could remember (or would admit to remembering) the following day. Thankfully a taxi home and then my weary little legs were snugly tucked up in bed. My thoughts inevitably drifted back to the film and the epic journey undertaken by those three young girls. Why was I grumbling about aching limbs?

As my slumbering thoughts drifted to what I had seen at the cinema, I determined to read the book. Then, having seen the film and read the book I knew that my choice of dissertation subject was right. *See, travel was still broadening my mind...*

Wednesday 24th April: sunny day for my Sydney Harbour Bridge Climb

Christmas present day! Once again up early and back down into town across the now familiar territory of Hyde Park to The Rocks, where I undertook my usual circumnavigation of a new area as I struggled to locate the entrance to the Bridge Climb. Finally found it and discovered I was thirty minutes early so had time to cool down. Obviously you don't just saunter out onto the bridge so a fairly lengthy induction process had to be gone through, including pulling on an attractive grey navvies overall and making sure that nothing was going to fall off my person or be spat out of my mouth. Twelve people every ten minutes go though a similar routine: every year thousands of small, grey crawling ants make the journey.

Although the climb is not strenuous, I was concerned that the dull hazy start to the day was not heralding ideal conditions for taking in the view. Off we set, in a line, and I was no longer looking at the sky but focussing on the solid structure as we temporarily disappeared from view. The first *wow* moment came as we emerged from one of the four enormous concrete supporting 'skewbacks' or piers and stepped out onto the steel frame of the bridge with traffic whizzing by rather close to my shoulder. As the climb progressed the sun obligingly burnt off the haze and we crested the summit in brilliant sunshine and what a breathtaking view! The harbour stretched out in all directions and the sea twinkled below us as tiny ferries ploughed backwards and forwards from bay to bay. For fear that someone might drop something onto the heads passing below, cameras are not permitted but of course the Bridge Climb has taken care of that by allowing the guides, Lance in our case, to photograph us solo and as a group. I did buy a couple – one because of the fabulous view of the harbour skyline and one of me beaming happily... which is in sharp contrast to the few others of me all of which portray a large lady frowning, and in need of a more supportive brassiere. At the summit, Lance told us the anecdote of how they had found a supermarket trolley up there one day. They get everywhere!

The climb experience takes three hours and as I had already decided that I should see live koalas and kangaroos, followed the 'Christmas present' with a trip to the zoo. As soon as I was re-attired in my civvies it was back down to the quay and off to Taronga Zoo, last visited by me circa 1962. From memory, it was a time when no one who cared anything about social standing would have dreamt of venturing into Sydney unless be-hatted, be-stockinged and be-gloved: the passing of those days is unlikely to have been mourned by many.

Today it was a quick zap over the water I had so recently been looking down upon followed by a cable car ride to the top of the hill on which the zoo is built, giving the giraffes the best view in Sydney. On such a steep site, it makes sense to start at the top and meander down. So down I meandered, wondering if the bridge climb had been more strenuous that I'd thought. Possibly the heat of the day was sapping my energy as I was beginning to skirt past any enclosures that seemed depressingly small, where the inmates were panting listlessly. Hordes of small noisome children, again around my ankles, struck me as being on the wrong side of the fence. Am I beginning to sound a bit jaded? The hazy day having turned into a scorcher, I was panting as visibly as the animals. The kinks in my meandering route straightened out as I opted for a more direct descent, still ensuring that I saw live versions of native Australian wildlife. However, the nocturnal animals were, unsurprisingly, a bit difficult to see but could be heard scrabbling around in the very dark, dark. Thanks to New Zealand's Lost World, I know the feeling chaps!

Back to the quay and into a scrum which left me defeated and waiting for the next ferry – never a chore when there is so much watery activity to help wile away the minutes. Finally disembarking at Circular Quay I walked home as if retracing my daily commute. A final stint of ironing awaited me, followed by a cooling shower, a change of outfit and a taxi ride with Matt to the ANA hotel where Alice was waiting for us. Then it was up to the Blu Bar on 36 (as in the floor number) to sample the best cocktails in town whilst taking in the magical view of night-time Sydney. Having been ushered into pole panoramic window position by a kindly waitress, who obviously recognised the dynamics created by a visiting mum, this was certainly 'a room with a view'. Whilst the red, white and blue neon lights flickered across the night skyline (the only colours permitted), I sipped my Moscow Mule in utter contentment and chatted away about my wonderful morning treat of a birds-eye view of the city and harbour.

No time to relax, back down to the pavement and a taxi ride to the Boathouse restaurant on Blackwattle Bay for oysters, crab and swordfish. Didn't think that oysters were my thing, but the tiny Claire de Lune Sydney Rock oysters were a gastronomic revelation: creamy and moreish. I followed these petit morsels with a mud crab that was "big enough to saddle up and ride round the room" (*thank you, waiter*). It was a messy treat but oh, so sweet.

A truly memorable meal marked the end of a sublime stay in Sydney – I had loved every moment and my hosts had been generous and fun. Packing was a bit of a weepy affair.

Uluru: the Red Centre

Thursday 25th April: pop goes the pension pot – staying at the embarrassingly plush Desert Gardens

This would be the highlight within a trip full of highlights. My itinerary included a visit to the Red Centre to enjoy the Kata Tjuta Gorge Walk; watch Uluru (Ayer's Rock) change colour at sunset; walk around the base of this magnificently memorable monolith; feel a bit of a gooseberry (unplanned) at the romantic Sounds of Silence dinner under the stars, and finally watch Uluru change colour at sunrise. Trailfinders does have some very persuasive staff!

The day dawned with a sad goodbye to Matt and Alice and then a taxi to the airport, where it was absolute bedlam. The 25th is ANZAC day and a public holiday. The day commences at four-thirty with a dawn service held at the Cenotaph in St Martin's Place in Sydney. After the solemnity comes the revelry which begins and ends in the pubs where 'two up' (heads or tails) a gambling game, illegal for the rest of the year, is played. Everyone gets totally blotto and it would have been fun to have taken part although I wouldn't have been able to keep apace with the hardened Sydney drinkers and would probably have disgraced myself in some alcoholic way. Complete strangers would not want to hear an earnestly slurred version of my life story. So instead of working towards a hangover, I was soberly heading off to the Red Centre and Uluru – hard to stay sad for long under such circumstances.

Having elbowed my way through the milling crowds, the flight was comfortable and by one o'clock I was checked into a decidedly non-backpackers' accommodation suffering from another severe attack of guilt... the room and the jaw-dropping view across to Uluru should really have been shared with my husband. Stoically, I sorted myself out and sallied forth on a trip to watch Uluru change colour as the sun sunk lower and lower chased by the ever-darkening sky. The Red Centre, home of this brooding sandstone formation, is really as red as it looks in photographs: stunning. My initial reaction upon seeing Uluru was that I wanted to get close to it and touch the surface; how warm was it – was it warm – surely anything that colour would be warm? But I would be coming back, so tonight I contented myself with just staring. It didn't take much imagination to understand why this landmark was sacred to the Anangu people. Uluru together with Kata Tjuta are owned by the Anangu who lease the area in which they stand to the National Park.

The trip also included a visit to Kata Tjuta, an awe-inspiring many-domed rock formation which is just as spell-binding as its more famous neighbour. We walked through the first section of the Valley of the Winds, where I think the daytime temperature can frequently soar above 36 degrees, making it unsafe for the average day-tripper tourist. Chatted to a fellow traveller who was from Mosman and had eaten at Lisa's, where I too had eaten. Here's a small puzzle, how did that connection get into our brief conversation? Irrespective of any commonality, he proceeded to make me a tad envious when describing his rather lovely job editing the *48 hours in...* publications which cover various parts of the world. Blithely, he added that not all his editorial efforts were confined to being desk-bound: lucky man!

Back at the hotel, I took stock of my surroundings and then pottered to a nearby supermarket where I bought a few bits and pieces to munch in my very luxurious, coolly green, room. There was no need to go 'out' for dinner my room was too comfortable to abandon.

Early to bed because...

Friday 26th April: an early start for a sunrise trip to Uluru

The early morning has a muffled quality and can feel quite chilly. Due to the dawn hour there was not much banter to be heard on the coach, as we were ferried out towards a viewing platform positioned far enough away from Uluru to allow us to scan the whole enormous bulk without craning our necks. We took up our positions and waited as the first rays of the sun began to creep above the horizon. Although yesterday I recorded the stunning red colour of Uluru, I'm not sure if on some days the changing colour as the sun rises (or sets) is more dramatic than on other days and whilst 'yes' the colour did this morning change from deep ochre to increasingly lighter ochre it wasn't quite as dramatic as I was expecting. Irrespective of my colour expectations, Uluru's sheer bulk at a height of 340 metres and a circumference of approximately 9.5km, creates a mightily awesome sight... and one which exerts an emotional tug that is hard to fathom. Simply, it's something visceral.

Out of respect for the Anangu people, I opted not to climb their sacred site and instead strode out to circumnavigate the base. Just a moment, would I under any circumstances scramble to the top? *Err, no.* The plaques remembering those whose climb was their final adventure hinted at a less altruistic reason for staying firmly on the ground. So around the base I went.

I think I must have chosen to walk in the opposite direction to everyone else as I walked alone except when passing people walking towards me. I eavesdropped on a couple of tourist guides as they explained the cultural significance of various rifts, gullies and Dreamtime rock paintings to their yawning audiences and watched the antics of some rather large lizards. Did I really expect to feel an electrical charge fizz through my body when I ran my hand across the surface of this sacred rock? Nothing. No wait, perhaps I did detect just the tiniest tingle of energy. On I walked, the earlier chill having been chased away by the morning sun. Stupidly it had not occurred to me to kit myself out with water, hat or snack. Fortunately, had I keeled over someone would eventually have stumbled across my prostrate body. Although I was in the middle of nowhere, thanks to tourism I would never be truly alone.

Having completed the circuit I wandered into and out of the deserted cultural centre, unfortunately not one of the park's greatest assets. Outside, in contrast, was buzzing. A three-day spirituality conference was being held at the Red Centre and the area was full of wafty, floaty hippie types wafting and floating around. The location had been chosen because of the spirituality of Uluru itself, plus the timing coincided with the full moon which also coincided with Buddha's birthday: three significant reasons. To complete the picture, the sight of a few psychedelic camper vans lazily bumping along sandy tracks added a 1960s Summer of Love dimension to the desert: unexpected and fun.

Amid all this spirituality and nostalgia taking place in an area known geologically (and incongruously) as the Amadeus Basin, I did wonder what the formations towards which we were all being drawn... actually were. Further scrutiny of signs and information told me that Uluru is arkose, a course-grained sandstone rich in the mineral feldspar. Whilst the 'plum pudding' shapes of Kata Tjuta are a conglomerate, comprised of basalt and granite pebbles, cobbles and boulders cemented together by sand and mud. Over an estimated period of 700 million years erosion caused by wind, weather and water has helped create these awe-inspiring shapes. Iceberg-like, much of these formations remain buried under the red desert sand.

Returning to the hotel, I chatted to Matilda as she tidied my room and then had a bite to eat before flopping in a rather hot and sweaty heap. Not sure how high the thermometer had climbed between sunrise and early afternoon but lethargy indicated that the ascent had been steep. And it was only in this comatose state that I registered the significance of the chambermaid's name. I hope people don't start whistling or waltzing in her presence.

When I originally worked out my itinerary I made choices based on cost as well as prioritising what I wanted to do and in amongst the 'not to be missed' slipped a few 'sounds good' without thinking the trip through. One such excursion was a dinner under the night sky, entitled the *Sounds of Silence*. Who would want to miss that?

Early that evening, I clambered aboard another coach and swiftly registered that I was a lone singleton. Of course, this was a romantic evening under the stars. The now full coach had taken its time doing the rounds to collect couples from various pick-up points and so the sun had almost set as we headed back out into the desert. Night fell swiftly and the view from the coach windows was black. At our destination we emerged to find tables set out under the rising moon: a more romantic spot it would be difficult to find. A glass of sparkling wine and canapés broke the ice whilst we were serenaded by a chap playing the guitar. A change of instrument to the didgeridoo changed the atmosphere of the evening... we really were in the Australian outback. Then to our tables, I joined couples from Sydney, Dublin and Chiswick... the west London couple I had already chatted to whilst sipping wine. The eighth member of the party was the coach driver: my partner for the evening!

At our table, I learnt that the husband from Chiswick was on a lecture tour as he kept asking his wife what the subjects were this time. I'm not sure that his forgetfulness bode too well for his forthcoming audiences but his wife reminded him firmly that this time it was art – circa nineteenth and twentieth centuries. From the way she spoke it wasn't clear if the subject or the dates were in question: surely not art one year and astrophysics the next? Mr and Mrs Chiswick and the alliterative David and Deidre from Dublin had a mutual friend: the St Ives artist Anthony Frost (so art was the correct topic). I looked blank at the name and was not helped when Mr Chiswick described the red and black splodgy souvenirs in the Royal Academy gift shop as being reproductions of his work. No, I was none the wiser... although now I am. I returned home and did my research and became familiar with the work of Anthony Frost and found that I was drawn to the boldly coloured abstract shapes he paints. The strong shapes and pure heat of his chosen palette sing to me of the Australian outback, the *never never*. I couldn't have been in a more appropriate spot to hear about the art of Anthony Frost. Perfect.

After a dinner of pumpkin soup (it works better in soup than on a pizza), plus bits of the animals I was struggling to see alive – crocodile, kangaroo and emu – with chicken for the less adventurous, assorted salads, macadamia pie, coffee and port it was lights out and settle back to listen to a spellbinding mother of six teenagers describe what we were sitting under but couldn't see because of cloud cover and a full moon. *Aarrgh.* In a lilting voice, which after that feast could so easily have lulled us to sleep, our astral guide took us on a journey across the skies, pointing out what could be seen of Orion, his belt and his two dogs. David made "I'm impressed" noises in my direction as I'd already pointed out the constellation to him (it's the only one I know, but I kept that bit quiet).

Next came the Southern Cross and its 'pointers' alpha and beta Centauri. A close neighbour of the Southern Cross, the Diamond Cross, was also visible and it was easy to see why the two constellations get muddled. The Australian flag is the Southern Cross and a mythical star. Next we were shown how to find due south, not as easy as in the northern hemisphere with the north, or pole, star: fascinating. I decided there and then that I should invest in an astral atlas. (Eventually I got an astral app, which I think I can make sense of… but gosh, what a lot of stars there are). Then we enjoyed a trip through the astrological calendar with as many constellations as possible being pointed out – from memory only Leo and Virgo were clearly discernable. It seemed wrong to wish that it hadn't been a full moon but the light was just too bright to make it a top notch star spotting night. Nevertheless, the evening was completely magical.

We returned to the hotel in time for a ten o'clock sociable nightcap; being a lone gooseberry had not been an issue. The evening was truly special. It was fun and informative and I was happily relieved that my companions had been both interested and interesting. Yes, travelling on your own is absolutely fine and that particular excursion gets a great big 'tick'. I'm so relieved that I didn't discard it as an unwanted romantic option.

… Relieved it was outside my room and not in it…

Ambling back to my room, I was halted in my tracks by the sight of a huge spider waiting expectantly in her equally huge, but scruffily straggly, tree-spanning web. I think I was looking at a female Golden Orb Weaver spider (aren't they bigger than the males?) but my ability to recognise spiders from pictures is as good as my ability at identifying plants and birds, and this one was certainly a hand-span or two bigger than the one I'd seen in Sydney. Whatever it was, I felt it necessary to tip-toe past quietly, relieved that it was outside my room and not in it.

Perth and North

Saturday 27th April: off to Perth and Western Australia for even more adventures, but not before...

Five in the morning and another early rise to again watch the sun strike the bulk that is Uluru. As we drove out into the desert, the moon that I had watched rising last night had almost completed its arc and was slowly dipping towards the distant horizon. Tumbling out at the viewing spot the chill in the air caused a sharp intake of breath: the weather was not as good as yesterday and there were many more tourists all vying for the best viewing spot. I took a few more photos of Uluru and again tried to see more in the changing colour than was actually visible. Have now decided that the shift through the spectrum of ochre is almost incidental as, whatever the shade, it is the sheer awe-inspiring bulk of this solitary monolith which magically lures the never sated photographer. On the way back to the hotel I spotted a lone dingo – as red as the Red Centre. Apparently true dingoes are solitary hunters but they will mate with any dog and it's the resultant feral breed that is the troublesome pack animal. This was one of my first native sightings that wasn't either lying sunny-side up or enclosed behind bars: *result*!

Another leg of my journey was coming to a close and once

again I packed George ready for the next adventure. Having checked out and bid farewell to my spider and Deidre and David, I spent a couple of hours wandering around the Ayers Rock shopping centre where I had raisin toast and coffee for breakfast, collected another two sets of photographs and made the odd purchase, including Neville Shute's *A Town Like Alice*... a town which was a mere 440km away. Then time to catch the transfer bus back to tiny Ayers Rock airport for the Qantas BAe 146 flight to Perth.

As I peered from the aircraft window, the enormity of the Red Centre really struck home as the desert sand with its smattering of salt pans remained visible virtually until touch-down at Perth. Australia is vast and I was about to spend time in its largest state: Western Australia. Referred to (unsurprisingly) as the 'Big State', Britain and Europe could sit comfortably within its borders. Geographically, this huge slice of Australia is sandwiched between the sparkling Indian Ocean along its western shore and an immense sandy nothingness to the east. A long way from anywhere, the benefit of this isolation is that it has helped to preserve unique plants and animals (how many would I see?) And the shoreline changes from the green and rocky southern capes to the smooth sandy beachscapes up beyond Perth (these I would surely see). My exploratory appetite had been whetted... and I would certainly experience the feeling of being 'a long way from anywhere'.

But first of all, welcome to the state capital. Arriving at Perth I found an airport only slightly larger than the one I had just left. Changed some money and managed to get a better rate than I had done in Sydney (I think) and then took a taxi into town. *Wow!* Did the driver talk so much to all his fares? It certainly wasn't a conversation, it was a no time to draw breath monologue: of Goan descent, his number one son is an engineer searching the world for new sources of oil and making a mint; number two son works for Accenture and is also making a mint; his (the driver's) brother lives in Sevenoaks, Kent where he is a shipping magnate and multimillionaire whose number one son is also making a mint but not in shipping, although he is about to go into shipping; number two son is a barrister... not sure about his pecuniary success. My driver is sixty-three years old and had been a pilot before moving into air traffic control and in his retirement he is now a taxi driver. His wife is of Canadian/Indian descent and has curly auburn hair and their number one son looks Greek. He showed me family photos – was he watching the road? I certainly saw an emu or two scuttling out of our way. He pointed out the Birdswood Casino and said that it was very respectable and therefore would be alright for me to have a flutter. He usefully described how to get to the best eateries and said *umm* the Ibis was clean but that was its sole recommendation. *Phew!*

Saying cheerio to my new friend, I checked into the Princes Ibis on Murray Street and, surveying my surroundings, thought that to award it one star was being generous: my taxi driver's lack of enthusiasm was probably not misplaced. In reality, the hotel proved to be more than adequate and (predictably) I soon found my way to the laundry room where I assessed the facilities with a now practised eye. As usual, the washing ritual required much energetic darting backwards and forwards to my room, as I lay claim to an empty machine, gathered the right coins, sorted my clothes into piles and bought a cup of washing powder with my dwindling small change. My room was quite a distance from the laundry room but when the bedroom floor shook I thought, *Aah, final spin...* and I was right. Hope those below the laundry paid a reduced room rate. There's nothing sophisticated about the Australian washing machines, they are usually top loaders with hot, warm, cold options and that's about it but they do work extremely well. Perhaps if my luggage had consisted of fewer books and more clothes, I might have spent less time carrying out a comparative study of laundry facilities and more time actually reading...

With today's laundry once again draped attractively around my room with perfected doss-house panache, it was time for a call home plus a chat with Matt who, in Sydney, was two hours ahead time-wise. Apparently Friday had been a bit of a struggle after an excellent and boozy ANZAC day. He was currently in the doghouse as he'd lost Alice's party clothes whilst tidying up. With her birthday falling mid-week, they were just about to set off for her party at a pub we'd visited with a delightful and cosy garden tucked away at the bottom of a short flight of steps. Re-reading this, I assume/hope Alice was either reunited with her party outfit or a suitable alternative was soon found. Anyway, whilst they went off to party the night away, I chowed-down on a couple of lamb chops and then went to bed after a preliminary saunter around the block to get my Perth bearings.

Murray Street proved to be an ideal central location, especially as that part of the city was constructed on a grid system making navigation a doddle, but the buildings immediately left and right of me were far from glamorous and a tiny bit seedy. *Surely I was not passing ladies of the night…?*

Sunday 28th April: back in true tourist mode, joining an organised trip…

… to cruise down the Swan River to Fremantle, visit the heritage markets, admire the city's architecture, drive along 'Millionaires Row' and back into Perth through King's Park. But first, the bells…

Gosh Perth is quiet. Saturday night didn't have much bustle so Sunday morning was bound to be even quieter. Wandered around the main sights on St George's Terrace and then visited the Swan Bell Tower which now houses the twelve 18th-century bells which once rang out across London from St Martin's-in-the-Fields and are immortalised in the *Oranges and Lemons* nursery rhyme: "You owe me five farthings say the bells of St Martins..." Parting with a few dollars, the leaflet I was given described how the bells had been rung in London in 1771 to celebrate Captain Cook's homecoming after his first voyage of discovery, having made landfall at Botany Bay in 1770. Records show that the bells were in existence before the 14th century and recast in the 16th and 18th centuries. They are one of the few sets of royal bells and are the only ones known to have left England. The biggest beast is the 1726 tenor bell which weighs a hefty 1,480kg.

With unusual good luck, they were being rung which unexpectedly made me feel a tiny bit nostalgic and rather a long way from home: a cousin was a member of St Martin's 'scrub club' which prepares the crypt morning and night for homeless people to find food and shelter... a long and valued St Martin's tradition. This was the only time in all my travels that could qualify as being labelled 'homesick': the moment in Melbourne doesn't count as it was cold sore induced.

... I shot up to the angels with both feet dangling...

Putting aside my leaflet, I listened as the bells were put through their Dixons, Dodges and Double Bob paces. Naturally, as a campanologist virgin I had to have a go. Joining a small band of fellow tourists I quickly mastered (after a fashion) the treble bells and when (another) Deidre asked if anyone would like to have a go at the 728kg bass beastie, of course I volunteered. Applying my new-found treble skill to this monster required some red-faced heaving but the clapper remained mute whilst I shot up to the angels with both feet dangling, cartoon-like, above the thigh-slapping audience gathered below. Descending from my impromptu vaudeville act I felt as if every one of my long-suffering vertebrae was now a good two inches from its nearest neighbour. Deidre no longer looked like a nice little lady, more a sadistic menace. She retrieved the bell rope from my shaking hands and with a nonchalance which set my teeth on edge proceeded to gently tweak the rope until the bell began to respond with a silent to and fro motion. As soon as the bell began to swing to Deidre's satisfaction, she smoothly pulled down and away went the bell – booming out its magnificent basso profondo voice. I'm just glad I wasn't given the tenor bell to play with…

Next I wandered, or limped, around taking photos of buildings that were rather finer than those close to my Murray Street accommodation, before settling down by the Swan River with a flat white, which then was a relatively new coffee phenomenon. Mulling over the majesty of some of the buildings I had been looking at, I appreciated that their construction had been made possible by the influx of convict labour. By the 1850s the struggling incoming free settlers realised that help was needed if the country was to grow and flourish. Known as 'ticket-of-leave' men, British convicts worked on projects integral to the development of agriculture, shipping and the state's infrastructure. They also constructed the historic buildings (both in Perth and Fremantle) I had been looking at.

It was within these cities fine walls that an economy and state legislature had begun to emerge as Western Australia moved towards becoming the state I was enjoying today.

As one o'clock approached, I ambled back to the hotel in time to join a tour of the Swan River and Fremantle. To begin with I was befriended by Tom and Peggy, Christian Malays from Kuala Lumpur. And as we edged away from our mooring, Peggy started talking to me, and continued without pausing for breath for the entire seventy-five minute cruise (Tom was rather good looking and I imagine very kind and patient). The conversation or monologue, the second I had listened to in two days, was surprisingly personal and not quite what I had expected to hear on a tourist trip – perhaps 'women's bits' will suffice as way of explanation.

In addition to the blush-worthy content, the monologue ranged over (in random order) tales of their two children both of whom had studied for their master's degrees in London at UCL; lost baggage; the role of Muslim women in Malaysia; religion in general; Mount Kinabalu; the weather in England; world travel and on and on… which is why I have the grand total of one photo with which to recall the journey. In reality, much of the conversation was very interesting but it was simply a case of the wrong time and place and also proved that I am hopeless at deflecting people from their conversational missions.

We disembarked to spend thirty minutes or so in the Fremantle Market Hall, the stalls were eclectic whilst the listed late Victorian building was a prestigious reminder of a bygone heyday. If what was under the roof was a slight disappointment, the striking roof itself was not and certainly ticked the tourist sight-seeing box. The market has undergone renovation and reinvention and I think the aim is to ensure that there is something for both residents and tourists alike. Possibly the plastic gewgaws aimed at the tourists were not quite what the average tourist really had in mind. I didn't feel compelled to part with my dollars. (I'm just beginning to wonder if I should track down a *pro bono* legal bod…)

Visit over and a coach ride took us back to Perth along roads which, according to our guide, best displayed Fremantle's unique Victorian interpretation of classical architecture. Here we looked at the city's grand civic buildings. Again, these handsome sandstone neo-classical structures provided further examples of 'ticket-of-leave' labour. In contrast, the *fin de siècle* public buildings, such as the P&O Hotel, carried with them a romantic echo of the US Mid west. Gazing at their intricate wrought-iron balustrades and balconies, I was transported to the gold-rush era of classic Westerns. Irrespective of the accuracy of the architectural analogy, my mind kept imagining Gary Cooper and Grace Kelly in scenes from *High Noon*.

The mood of romanticism continued as we dove on to admire the predominantly 1980s 'Millionaire's Row' confections, these statement homes hug the northern banks of the Swan River. An abundance of banksias in full colourful flower added a further touch of theatricality to this part of the city. Here you find addresses such as Peppermint Grove and Matilda Bay where the architectural mix, river frontage and manicured gardens indicate hefty price tags.

The route into Perth continued through King's Park and Botanic Gardens from where you get the most stunning views across the city. Out came the camera and I was able to make up for having missed out on the earlier river-trip photo opportunities. This tantalising first glimpse of the park ensured that it was re-visited before flying off to Tokyo. King's Park is another premier example of Australia's botanical gardens and not to be missed.

Back at the hotel, my two early mornings caught up with me and I intended to have an early night, but flicking through the TV channels, the *Pop Star Solo* final caught my eye. At some previous point I had channel-flicked and spotted the programme when they were down to the last four contestants and now it was the final pair. The girl who won was reasonable but I was rooting for the boy who I felt had the potential to bring in the pennies for whoever managed him: right chap, outdoory Aussie with strong voice but wrong song. *Hey ho*!

Monday 29th April: A trip north to Coral Bay via Monkey Mia

The independent traveller has now fully morphed into a coach passenger as I embark upon the 'Five Day Pinnacles Tour' from Perth to Coral Bay via the dolphins at Monkey Mia and the clear waters of Ningaloo reef. But first of all...

... a few more Perth facts: the concert hall has the best acoustics in Australia although from the outside the concrete Brutalist form is considered by some to be uninviting (it opened in 1973, the same year as the architecturally more challenging and eye-appealing 'shell' structure of Sydney Opera House). During the reign of Queen Victoria when Perth was taking shape and expanding 'someone' decreed that when naming the roads if a road bearing the monarch's name cut across another road, the non-monarch road had to change its name at the point of intersection. For example, St George's Terrace continues as Adelaide Terrace at the junction with Victoria Street. The road tunnel built to bypass the city of Perth is the only road tunnel in Western Australia. Perth proudly asserts that its soccer team, Perth Glory, is one of Australia's leading teams (but a little research reveals a chequered history, although it has won three Premierships since its formation in 1995).

And there's more. In 1829, following the explorations of Captain Sir James Stirling who had been seeking fresh water and suitable anchorage to support the establishment of a British colony, the spot chosen was named Guildford and became the centre of the Swan River Colony, until Perth became the more dominant city. Although born in Scotland, Sir James died at his home in

Guildford, Surrey. Lilac Hill cricket ground hosts the first match for the visiting English team every time they play in Australia. *You'll thank me* – that has to crop up in a pub quiz, surely?

The Swan Valley, an area renowned for the production of white Burgundy and fortified wine, is home to several boutique wineries with restaurants attached plus a growing number of microbreweries. The Y frames on which the vines are grown exposes the fruit more fully to the sun allowing for maximum absorption of the sun's rays. This, combined with the late harvest, provides the ideal base for fortified wine. The constant shortage of water in the region has led to ever more resourceful ways to trickle feed the roots of the plants minimising loss of water through evaporation. Unrelated, an early victim of colonisation, the Western Swamp Turtle had been thought to have become extinct until the 1940s when a child brought a turtle into school and the reptile's colony was subsequently found. The Swamp Turtle is once again thriving. There are lots of studs around the Perth area, with lovely gleaming brood mares.

The Brand Highway which connects Perth to Geraldton and on to Port Headland, is an 1800km section of the world's longest highway, Highway 1, which circumnavigates Australia over a total distance of 14,500km. Depending upon the importance of the section, it is designated M1, A1 or B1 as around you go. If you drive the western section in an anti-clockwise direction you have to add 64km. Much of the highway is single track. Just north of Perth, 36.5 metre road trains assemble at Bullsbrook, on their way to Carnarvon where they are permitted to increase to 53.5 metres and beyond Carnarvon they haul 65 metres… if one comes towards you on a single track section of Highway 1, no points for guessing which of you hits the dust. 'Free coffee for driver' signs herald the approach of welcoming watering and fuel stops.

Okay, so where is all this information coming from? The running commentary provided by our knowledgeable guide,

Hans, on the coach drive north as we bowl along towards
Monkey Mia. Through my window on the world (hooray, I
have an empty seat next to me so I can sprawl with ease) I am
gazing transfixed by the vastness of the landscape; if I thought
I had seen large landscapes before, well, I was mistaken… they
just seem to get bigger and bigger. At the moment, the road is
running parallel to a slight ridge and to my left, in front, behind
and beside are small trees scattered amid a pale green landscape
and it has been like this for mile after mile. The small trees share
their space with lots of banksias named after Joseph Banks, the
botanist aboard Captain Cook's *Endeavour*. Just like the South
African Protea, they need bushfires to burn open the seed casing
allowing germination to occur. Standing dwarfed against the
expansive outback the once named 'Blackboy' monocots, now
known as grass trees, do indeed look like sentries guarding
sacred tracks with their short trunks and grassy topknots (their
new name is as original as the New Zealand tree fern).

We pass a titanium oxide and zircon mine from which the
standard 2.5km rail trains haul the minerals from the interior
mine site up to the coast at Port Dampier. Hans continues to
be a human mine of information as we pass Rio Tinto's Argyle
Diamond Mine, which happens to be the world's largest supplier
of coloured diamonds: 90 percent of the world's pink diamonds
are extracted here plus champagne, cognac and rare blue. These
are auctioned in Switzerland in sealed bids. However, 94 percent
of the output is of industrial quality. Apparently, the Australian
government will not allow de Beers to buy into the operation.
And of course, not too many hundreds of kilometres away are
the mega gold mines at Kalgoorlie-Boulder: Western Australia
sits on an abundance of mineral wealth.

[Years of taking cramp-inducing long-hand minutes in the
charity world have obviously been of benefit: re-reading my
notes I'm impressed I had any time to notice the view.]

Lunch today was taken by the water's edge in the rock

lobster fishing port of Port Denison. The water in the harbour was crystal clear and I salivated at the thought of freshly caught sweet lobster. The earlier coffee stop was unmemorable or perhaps memorable for the wrong reasons: grotty loos and coffee in polystyrene cups, I don't think the average driver would have relished the 'free drink' offer.

Four hundred kilometres north of Perth we stop to look at one of the main tourist attractions on this stretch of road: the arthritic leaning trees of Greenough. Looking like ancient decrepit elders these trees, Red River Gums, are bent at a dramatic 90 degrees to the ground their trunks bowed at this seemingly impossible angle due to the consistently strong salt-laden coastal winds... which were inconsistently absent during our visit. As expected, we all took photographs, but I purposely waited until there was no one in sight before taking mine. *Umm*, sometimes, human interest helps to give an idea of scale...

By now the weather was getting warmer and the scenery beginning to look a bit déjà vu, so I caught up with my journal and read a few more chapters from *A Town Like Alice*. By four o'clock and nearing the end of our 900km drive, I registered the fact that we were back in a red sand environment where the straggly gum trees bore signs of bark damage caused by roaming herds of cattle and sheep. All around was scrub – stunted trees, red sand, blue skies across which drifted enormous grey clouds: wonderful! Perhaps I suffer from claustrophobia... I had no idea lots of empty nothingness would be so appealing.

The coach continued to trundle along the Brand Highway north to the Peron Peninsula and the region of Shark Bay where we spent the night at Monkey Mia. All along the coast you glimpse water that is crystal clear and sapphire blue: the holiday brochure pictures hadn't lied.

Obviously recording Hans' words of wisdom caused a return of writer's cramp as I have no note of where we stayed or how sociable we were with our eating arrangements. Having spent time with chatty taxi drivers and chatty tourists, it seems my fellow coach travellers were rather more subdued. Or maybe my head-down scribbling made me seem a bit aloof.

Tuesday 30th April: bottlenose dolphins versus peckish pelicans

Onwards from Monkey Mia to Carnarvon along the Coral Coast. Although I got up early, I unintentionally managed to miss the sunrise. Walked down to the water's edge to find tourists lined up ready for the highlight of the day: to interact with families of wild bottlenose dolphins. This activity has been taking place for twenty-five years. In fact, three dolphins are fed daily from a school of about thirty which lives out in the bay. Only females are fed and I thought the guide said that the same three are fed…but that seems a bit mean although it would be a way of ensuring that the entire school does not become reliant on handouts. The males are too aggressive to be fed, but didn't think to ask what happens if they turn up uninvited to the breakfast table. It is possible to stroke the dolphins, but I prissily declined as that seemed a bit too circusey.

Inevitably, free fishy handouts are going to attract other piscine loving creatures and sure enough the pelican sideshow going on behind the wall of tourists was equally compelling to watch. Pelicans have to be kept at a distance from the dolphins' breakfast for fear that they would break up the party. So a chap waving a blue bucket out of which he occasionally extracts a morsel of fish keeps the birds busy as they jostle and dance in the hope that a fishy morsel will come their way. So my dilemma was one of which way to face? Was it to be seawards and the rather tame wild dolphins or landward and a group of jostling jumping pelicans? The pelicans just edged the vote. What characters! I left the fishy feast to stroll along the beach before heading back to the coach for a ten-fifteen departure for Shark Bay.

... Jostling, jumping... The pelican sideshow...

The Shark Bay region is vast within an area of vastness and the first stop was Denham a small town with a resident population of a little over 600. However, the numbers swell each year with the influx of tourists into the region all intent on visiting the town famed for being the most westerly accessible town in Australia. Denham is not just famed for its location, but also for its older houses which are built from compacted cockle shells, as was the restaurant where we stopped for a delicious crayfish lunch.

Our après lunch destination was Shell Beach, the source of the building material. On the way we stopped at Eagle Bluff, a high cliff which overlooks the Denham Sound waters of Shark Bay. The view was breathtaking, the water was so blue and so clear and the black shapes soon revealed themselves to be rays drifting and gliding without causing even the tiniest of ripples. Sharks, dolphins and dugongs also inhabit the waters, but sadly they were not putting in an appearance for our benefit. Similarly, whale sharks cruise the shoreline and although they can grow to a staggering 20 metres, the world's largest known fish is a gentle giant of the sea. Even so, I'm not sure how I would react if 20 metres of fish came to investigate my mask and snorkel as did the Cook Island minnows. That's wrong, I know exactly how I would react... Turning away from the sea and my aquatic ruminations, glistening salt pyramids were visible on the horizon marking the site of solar evaporation salt works.

Back on the coach, barely one third full, we all kept ourselves to ourselves which, on this occasion, really suited me as the scenery was far too mesmeric to warrant chit chat. The next leg took us to the incredible 110km of Shell Beach; one of only two beaches in the world made entirely from cockle shells (I think you'll find the other one in Florida). Over the millennia the shells have become compacted, up to a depth of ten metres, to form a limestone known as coquina, a material that was mined in block form for the construction of the buildings in Denham. Mining stopped when the beach became a World Heritage Site, although small amounts can still be extracted to repair and conserve the original buildings. You need your sunnies... as the billions of tiny white shells which stretch for as far as the eye can see twinkle with a bright luminescence in the sunlight. The crystal clear Indian Ocean sighs gently against these tiny shells with a watery whispered breath. It is the sort of place that travellers stumble upon, hang up their rucksacks and decide to go no further. Although tempted, and George wouldn't have complained, we continued north as there was still more to see.

The next stop was Hamelin Pool, to see stromatolites the oldest and largest living fossils on earth. These innocuous water-bound blobs play an important role in helping scientists to understand the Earth's evolution. What we were gazing at is thought to represent what life on earth looked like 3.5 billion years ago. Hamelin Pool is one of only two places where these living marine fossils exist and the high salinity of the water allows them to grow undisturbed by predators. Here, the salty soup occurs due to the position of a sandbar across the entrance to the bay. This natural barrier preserves a shallow sea-water pool, from which the water evaporates swiftly. The resulting increase in saline levels allows these weird ancestral specimens to flourish. *Are they the reason why I love being in water?* Although the stromatolites are not predated upon, man has managed to leave his mark. Today boardwalks protect the living fossils but as you peer down you can see traces of cart tracks left over sixty years ago by wool wagons taking cargo out to waiting ships. Then, amid all this pre-history speculation about my antecessors, my camera battery ran out.

Landwards, scanning the barren terrain, I was surprised to learn that the sparse vegetation does in fact support a large number of feral goats, escapees from earlier days. These animals are culled from time to time and their meat sold to Muslim countries. I didn't ask if the meat was halal, but I suppose that would be the case and I really hoped that carcasses were shipped and not animals, but I guess that would not be the case. An image of the Melbourne sheep transporter with under-slung dogs came to mind, it had been heading towards Avalon airport. With a small shudder that the realities of life can provoke, it was time to move on.

After an amazing day we finally rolled into Carnarvon, where our most northerly hotel was located. It's not the most exciting spot in Western Australia but it is the gateway to the glorious Ningaloo Reef, a 'fringing reef' where the coral starts at the water's edge. Here you are a brief snorkel and leg-kick away from thriving coral and all the communities that the coral supports. The buildings in the town are enhanced by scrambling bougainvilleas and lush hibiscus plants, with large baobab trees giving shade. Unsurprisingly, the tourist blurb makes no reference to the fact that Carnarvon is the Social Services town for the region. Unemployed indigenous Australians, who have lost any incentive to work due to decades of destabilisation of their communities, drift into town seeking handouts which then fund drinking binges. Those who become inebriated are locked up at night and shops have bars to keep shopkeepers and customers apart. It all seemed rather tragic, and I so hope that in the intervening years, life has become little better for the Yamtji people.

Sadly, the story should be different as the Carnarvon area

is made fertile by the waters of the Gascoyne River hence the region is known as the bread basket of Western Australia. Although there is little or no rainfall in the region, the river floods periodically from its source 600km away thereby enabling fruits such as paw paw, pineapple, melons and bananas to grow in abundance. For most of the year the river runs deep underground so the life-giving waters remain unseen.

The last jaunt of the day was a visit to the Westoby banana plantation once run by John Cleese, one of 180 plus such plantations in the region. On reflection, I'm not sure if I believe the John Cleese link as sitting here looking at the postcard of the current owner/manager Paul Nevill, he looks a tad like JC. Mr Nevill signed the postcard for me with 'G'Day Baby'... and "no" I don't think that was a unique 'just for me' form of address. Mr Nevill was a garrulous cheery man but it was a little hard keeping the ear to ear grin in place as he burbled away merrily about the joy of banana farming.

Oh, dear, my hotel room in Carnarvon was 1930s grim. The solid bars at the window made me feel that I was being kept in rather than interlopers out. But for one night, it didn't matter...

Wednesday 1st May: the month begins at Coral Bay

Coral Bay is the point at which Ningaloo Reef is closest to the shore making it one of the most accessible reefs in the world. A cruise, a snorkel, a turtle and lunch...

Back on the road, heading north, without a backward glance at sadly dreary accommodation and with camera battery charged and underwater camera at the ready. Our 'elevenses' stop for tea and cake was timed for our arrival at the Tropic of Capricorn, with usual photos taken of aged tourists jumping backwards and forwards over said invisible line. Arriving at our Coral Bay destination, a tiny settlement to which tourists are drawn, we hastily piled out of the coach and onto a rather rickety looking glass-bottomed boat. What a fabulous trip! Peering down, so many different corals revealed themselves seemingly millimetres away from the glass: brain, cabbage, antler, etc. Perhaps not overly colourful, but packed densely together the corals provide shelter for all manner of fish and a playground for rays and turtles.

And a playground for me! I couldn't resist! The Cook Islands seemed so long ago. Snorkel in place, I spent a blissful time wallowing in the water... all on my own except for the turtle which drifted along beside me as if sensing I needed company. No one else on the boat wanted to get wet. *What*? How many opportunities would there be to drift amongst some 220 species of coral and 500 species of fish? Ningaloo is without doubt spectacular. Of course I wish I'd seen a whale shark, although my reaction had this leviathan swam towards me would certainly have provided my ship-bound audience with an unscheduled slice of entertainment. With my audience in mind, I reluctantly said "cheerio" to my turtle and heaved myself back on board.

After lunch, I again took to the water pushing off from the sandy shore and felt oh so happy to be back in a marine wonderland. This time, others in our party joined me... it would have been weird if they hadn't: this was the purpose of all those hours on the coach. Eventually, with the watery business of the day concluded, we trundled back south with plenty of stops for the plentiful scenic photo opportunities. Some of the feathered wildlife proved too difficult to photograph, wedge tailed eagles, emus, lorikeets, parakeets and numerous galahs weren't interested in posing, so instead it was peaceful just admiring their antics. Sometimes it's better just to look and enjoy. And realistically, the open spaces presented my limited skills with too great a challenge. So I contentedly continued to gaze through my window on the world as on we rolled, until a particularly bleak vista came into view. All around the earth was scorched. An extensive blackened area disappeared over the horizon, the result of a devastating bush fire, on this occasion caused by careless individuals.

Hello... how remiss of me, I had forgotten... as Coral Bay was the most northerly point on our itinerary we had to turn around, head south, and at six o'clock in the evening here we are again, back behind bars in Carnarvon for the night...

Thursday 2nd May: from Carnarvon to Geraldton

Now it's time to bid farewell to Carnarvon, which sort of grew on me second time around. My guide books states that 'Carnarvon has few tourist pretentions', make of that what you will.

We continued our journey south to visit Kalbarri and explore the deep red river gorges of the Murchison River. The route followed the dramatic coastal cliffs and on the way I watched as wedge tailed eagles, Australia's largest bird of prey, caught the thermals and circled looking for food – or perhaps simply having fun? I'd like to think that they were enjoying the moment. Lost in this reverie, I apparently missed assorted kangaroos and emus, except for one old veteran roo. There he was, just waiting for us to roll by, lolling beside the road amid mountainous termite mounds and eucalypts the colour of pretzels. *Thank you, sir!*

At some point we obviously arrived at our Geraldton destination, which is as the tourist information proclaims the area's largest town and Western Australia's major winter tourist resort. In addition, it is base for the multi-million dollar rock lobster industry and the local waters teem with fish.

Apart from that little snippet, my journal lay untouched... perhaps jotting down all that Hans told us, has taken its toll.

Friday 3rd May: this might be the last day on the tour bus, but...

... there is still a lot to see between Geraldton and Perth, including limestone spires resembling an eerie moon landscape.

I started the day proclaiming lots to see, but once again the pages of my journal lay undisturbed. Perhaps conversation was picking up on board the coach? What was memorable was the trip to see the Pinnacles. Turning slightly inland at the fishing port of Cervantes, we headed for the Nambung National Park. I had seen pictures of what I was about to view in person, but even so the dramatic limestone formations piercing through the burnished sand of gently undulating dunes was a breath-taking spectacle. The scattered shapes, some tall and slender others jagged and irregular, looked as if they had been arranged by man. Apparently in springtime the area abounds with flowers, but in the dry heat of May it was hard to imagine anything growing in such an arid spot. As a tourist attraction, the Pinnacles did not appear on the tourist circuit until the 1960s when the area became designated as a national park. That really wasn't very long ago.

All trip I have been keeping a sharp lookout for the iconic Western grey kangaroos but have failed to see much in the way of roo activity: yesterday's inert chap could easily have been a stuffed example to keep passing tourists, like me, happy. To rub salt into this particular wound we walked over virgin sand to get closer to the Pinnacles and then on turning to retrace our steps our footprints had been over-trodden by a large kangaroo. You turn your back for two minutes... how could I miss one again? And a large one at that? The best I could do was photograph a limestone formation which, uncannily, looked very much like yesterday's large specimen. The Western grey is common southwards from just below Shark Bay and although they remained uncommon as far as I was concerned, I forgive them as I do rather like their Latin name: *Macropus Fuliginosus*.

Macropus Fuliginosus

Back in Perth, I only vaguely remember saying "cheerio" to my travelling companions when I was dropped off at my hotel and I do hope that my thanks to Hans were earnest enough. Still a bit vague about 'what next', but knowing me, I spent the evening doing my washing. The bit I do remember is that George and I shared a very tiny basement room. Anyway, it really didn't matter because the next day I was off to Tokyo to catch up with Kevin, my amazingly tolerant and generous husband. Now it was his turn for some travel fun.

The next morning I phoned Matt from the airport and felt very sad to be leaving him and his diverse country of adoption. Now I could really understand why having travelled half way round the world he was currently showing no sign of completing his circumnavigation. On the up side, I was looking forward to seeing his sister in her new environment and sharing the Japanese journey with my husband... who I would probably bore to bits with tales of my adventures.

A day later, I landed at Tokyo's Narita airport and courtesy of Japanese efficiency, made my way effortlessly via public transport to the New Otani Hotel. Standing at the reception desk in the ultra-smart hotel lobby, I happened to glance down at my feet... the shoes which had caused problems all those weeks ago at Heathrow were once again flashing neon signs: I had transported an impressive quantity of the Nambung

National Park across the skies and was now leaving footprints on a pristine Japanese carpet. George too, showing signs of travel fatigue, seemed similarly to be letting the side down. Looking up sheepishly from this sandy tableau, the sight of a very tall European striding towards me across the crowded lobby banished all thoughts of the illegal cargo of sand on my shoes.

Reaching into my bag to dab on some perfume from the dregs of my much travelled bottle, I was metaphorically, if not actually, home.

Further Travels with George

... I raided the ever-more apprehensive piggy bank...

Some eighteen months later, a further opportunity arose to travel on my own with, once again, Sydney as the ultimate destination. My previous journey had whetted my appetite and I wanted to see more of Australia's rich diversity as I made my way towards the capital of New South Wales. Spoilt for choice, the Northern Territory, Queensland and unexplored tracts of Western Australia all beckoned. But what was feasible?

The goal was to spend a family Christmas in Sydney, and I would be the 'advance party'... but how 'advance' was not specified. So I pushed my luck by just happening to say in a vague way, "Wouldn't it be lovely to head off a little earlier to see a bit more of the country... perhaps mid-November might be a good time to go?" Somehow this suggestion got the thumbs up and once again I raided the ever-more apprehensive piggy bank and was on the phone to those helpful people at Trailfinders...

Having gone west from Heathrow last time, this time I travelled east choosing Kuala Lumpur for a brief stop-over. Was I subconsciously recalling the trip on the Swan River listening to Peggy as she chatted about life in this city? Whatever the reason, I didn't bother to consult the weather charts for KL, or for any of my itinerary, instead I just trusted to luck, packed a slightly grubby looking George and headed off.

Kuala Lumpur

Wednesday 19th November: here we go again...

The adventure begins with another early travel start and a dawn farewell to my kindly chauffeuring husband at Heathrow Terminal 4. Unlike my first trip, the check-in was smooth and swift allowing me one and a half hours to sort out my new mobile phone. Managed to keep the old number, but failed to ensure that I could phone home from distant lands. Seem to remember last time it was a new camera that caused constant technological stresses, so technology could become an over-used motif in my writing endeavours: will try to rein it in. Perhaps I should adopt the same discipline towards food?

Anyway, the flight was virtually full – mainly English rugby supporters heading for Sydney and doing their best to emulate the worst of English football fans. Fortunately I had one of the few empty seats next to me in a row of three which gave some welcome breathing distance between myself and a none too fragrant gentleman from Macclesfield. He had thought he would be sitting in an aisle seat but was allocated a window seat – not of his choosing. So before we had fastened our seat belts we had one unhappy passenger on board, he simmering by the window and me serenely on the aisle (the seat I had requested after my last loo-visiting shenanigans with the gentleman in 19B).

At one stage, between Mr Macclesfield's frequent trips to the loo I did offer half-heartedly to swap seats but he declined and stayed curled up by the window except when getting me to put up my tray table, untangle myself from the headphone cable and generally clear a safe passage so that he could get out (think an excess of beer could have been the root cause of all this to-ing and fro-ing). It seems that there are loo drawbacks irrespective of which seat you sit in. Unfortunately though, each time he got up he lent heavily on the back of the seat of the chap in front of him – who by about Istanbul was in a simmering rage, refusing to help matters by ensuring his own seat was as far back as possible, thereby making Mr Macclesfield's manoeuvring even more difficult. This finally got his goat and he flipped, ramming the intrusive seat forward with such a jolt that it must have been truly painful for the unrelenting "I've paid for my seat... I'll position it as I want" bloke in front.

My wimpish attempts as peace and reconciliation failed dramatically. Thankfully, sensing my discomfort, by approximately Nepal the Cabin Services Director magically managed to find a more spacious and secluded seat for Mr Macclesfield and I was left in peace, with a soothing gin and tonic. After the seat-ramming incident and before his relocation my neighbour had morphed from curled-up recluse into a non-stop chatterbox and I was beginning to mentally shout, "Enough!" As was the chap in front who continued to simmer in an obtrusive way. Not sure why, but I did feel a bit sorry for Mr Macclesfield, and did wonder how he got on during his stopover in Singapore prior to going down to Perth to visit his sister. For her sake, I hope he arrived sober.

As for me, I arrived at Terminal 1 in Singapore and transferred across to Terminal 2 and during the long trek felt that at least the exercise would diminish any chances of a deep vein thrombosis cutting short my vacation. More time was spent playing with my phone before embarking for the short flight to Kuala Lumpur and its elegant new airport. The 70km journey into the city centre was completed painlessly on a fast train and then a taxi took me to the Swiss Garden Hotel, chosen for its location in the centre of KL sandwiched between the hustle and bustle of Bukit Bintang and colourful Chinatown (an area in any city worth a visit).

Thursday 20th November: a case of jet lag

Feeling weary after a twenty-four hour travel extravaganza, with added seat-rage, my eager anticipation of flopping exhausted onto a bed, in a half-decent room, was a little bit crushed. Opening the door to my room, I heard myself let out an audible gasp as I surveyed my surroundings: it was an unexpected hovel. The room was drab and depressing and the air conditioning unit must have leaked badly at some stage as half of the wall in the lobby area was coming away and bits of ceiling were hanging down: charming. Back down to reception I trundled George, the trusty guardian of my possessions, where Janet appeared to be quite upset that I should consider one of her rooms to be 'dreadful'. Fortunately she agreed to move me without the need for a prolonged discussion to a room which was infinitely better. Although not exactly 5* it did at least appear to be structurally sound and I thought I would eventually get to grips with the temperamental kettle and why should I worry if the bath plug was useless?

A short snooze followed by a quick shower had the desired revivifying effect and I set off, out for a night on the town. Found a shopping plaza where I mooched around and bought a necessary umbrella before sauntering off in search of food, finally settling on noodles, duck with ginger and pak choi, in a basement noodle bar. I felt reasonably proficient as I tweezered up mouthfuls of pak choi and ginger with my chopsticks, but the duck was mainly bones and bits that were unfamiliar to my delicate Western palette so I wasn't really sure that I wanted to play chopsticks with them. I know slurping is the thing to do, but I did struggle with the noodles as they slopped and slithered around in the stock/gravy/soup which I tried hard not to splash all over the place, without much success as it was greasily dripping down my chin and onto the table. It was one of those meals where the sheer exertion of getting edible food into your mouth actually makes you hungrier and hungrier. The cool beer was happily manageable and very welcome. When the noodle struggle got too great (probably to watch) a spoon and fork appeared as if by magic! My first meal, with beer, in KL had cost the princely sum of 17 ringgits, which converts to just a little under £3… that's how we backpackers like to enjoy ourselves.

Sort of replete, I wandered out into the night under the shelter of my new umbrella and immediately thought that a bigger brolly would have covered everything and dark trousers wouldn't have shown the rain splatters quite like my light ones. I had forgotten how tropical tropical rain can be… raindrops like sharp silver bullets. Fighting off tiredness, I wandered a little longer before falling into the clutches of one of the shops in massage row. I thought that perhaps the foot reflexology might be just the thing to disperse any imagined signs of DVT (or perhaps, on reflection, it was the one activity guaranteed to shift any lurking blood clots in exactly the wrong direction… happily I'm still on my perch some twelve years later). Scrambling onto a rather grubby massage table I decided that my surroundings were not quite on a par with the Doha Ritz-Carlton (thank you Kate), but the ensuing pummelling and squeezing was equally effective: "Ooh-ouch, yes it hurts, but ignore my squeals, I'm sure… aaargh… it's good." So impressed was I by the fiver's worth of prodding that I splashed out another fiver for a head and back massage.

I floated back out onto the streets and into a clothes shop where I tried on an irresistible black outfit – cropped trousers and a slimming top – behind a tiny scrap of modesty curtain. For only a few ringgits more than my supper I made a purchase which lasted years and nearly made me weep when it finally fell to bits.

The feeling of euphoria continued as I made my way back to my room ready for bed and at midnight my massaged head finally hit the pillow. Drifting off to sleep I decided that KL was really rather okay.

Friday 21st November: a failed mission

I awoke to a grey morning with heavy clouds blotting out the view of the surrounding hills. Assessing the contents of my wardrobe, I decided to wear my walking shoes as last night's choice of flip-flops had exposed my toes to things they'd have been happier not exploring. The city, I had already discovered, is a mix of old and new jostling side-by-side. The old can look a little grubby and tatty but that's because the rain and high humidity does nothing for anything other than encourage black mould to creep over concrete buildings.

Setting off to explore, I spent an intellectual morning in the main building of the National Museum where the artefacts told the story of the customs, costumes and cultures of the diverse races which make up the Malaysian population. You did have to look past the rather moth-eaten mannequins but, once that was done, the information was illuminating. For example, did you know that there are 101 ways to fold a square of material to make the distinctive headwear worn by Malay men? Next I found the circumcision display luridly fascinating, and seemingly it too could be done in 101 ways. There was an eclectic selection of secondary exhibitions including some splendidly ornate gold which was part of a temporary exhibition of installations designed by a Mexican artist: the museum tried to link Malaysia and Mexico but apart from them both sharing the letter M, the link seemed rather tenuous.

The final exhibition was dedicated to marine salvage activities and that too was surprisingly interesting. There were reconstructions of rotting 17th-century hulks with rotting crates of broken cargoes of pottery. In amongst the broken pieces were acres and acres of delicate Chinese celadon (green ware) some of which had survived intact in superb condition but was now doomed to be immersed forever in water in the museum viewing tanks. Musical instruments, weaponry and (dry) ceramics completed the national collection.

After a wander around the grounds, I set off for the Central Station, a mission that was easier said than done as it seemed impossible to cross the maze of roads. Eventually I conceded defeat and asked directions which led me safely to the rear of the station. Having located myself, I was then able to head towards the Petronas Towers – this iconic structure being the main reason for choosing KL as a stopover: *homework, homework*. Presenting myself at the ticket office I learnt that trips to the top take place during the morning only and I had therefore arrived too late to make that all important journey skywards. My KL mission had failed! The first four floors plus the basement area house a gigantic, all too familiar, shopping complex: Laura Ashley, Body Shop, M&S... home from home really.

Feeling a little deflated I boosted my energy levels with a carrot and ginger juice and then, revived, discovered the most gigantic bookshop... surely on a global scale the biggest ever... with what appeared to be every publication in every language. Spent a few minutes in the English section playing "have they got…" and "yes" they had. My disappointment at not travelling to the top of the Petronas Towers melted away.

Made my way back to the hotel via, I thought, the Central Market but due to its rather low-key state was a little uncertain; nevertheless, what I was walking past gave me a glimpse into a colourful world and one that was busy, busy, busy. I finally stopped for a cool and refreshing beer in China Town, where I lounged contentedly in an old rattan chair and watched and listened as a polyphonic world pottered by. Reluctantly I vacated this comfortable vantage point and dawdled back to the hotel. By the time I reached my room, I felt weary with a tiny niggle of despondency at having failed in my KL mission. Not wishing to end the day on a negative note, I turned around and headed back into the busy streets and found a buzzing eatery where I sampled more Malaysian delights; the perfect antidote to boost my flagging spirits. Watching the comings and goings of local life combined with my second chop stick challenge ensured a happy evening.

Finally, bed beckoned so I wandered back to the hotel, crawled under the sheets where the sights, sounds and smells of KL whooshed around in my head chasing away all thoughts of unseen lofty views.

Saturday 22nd November: phew, it's hot

Early next morning, back again onto the streets of KL where *gosh* the humidity was already sweat-inducingly high. Managed an enervating amble towards the coach and taxi station and discovered the real Central Market where I made a few purchases and, in desperation, tackled an Asian loo. By now I should be au fait with squat loo etiquette but it does present a challenge or two… the greatest being keeping clothes out of the way of the floor. Enough of that – out on the road again I caught a taxi to the Lake Park and sat for longer than was comfortable in very heavy traffic (again, homework, homework): it was the end of Ramadan and everyone was heading out of the city on a five day holiday.

The journey might have taken longer than anticipated, but the location did not disappoint. As expected, large-leafed tropical plants filled the beautifully landscaped park plus orchids and a butterfly house into which I wandered. In said house, I think I may have inadvertently reduced the number of inmates by one, either that or the butterfly was feeling as exhausted as I was, as there it lay in a crumpled heap at my feet, its magical colours slowly fading as its life-force seeped away. I really hope I wasn't the culprit but no one else was near me at the time the murder was committed... I guess I just trod on the resting lepidopteron. *Sorry*. Whilst this little drama was being played out, its other more savvy relations were keeping well away from me but in doing so were putting on the most glorious display. Butterflies the size of songbirds flitted from lush flower to lush flower and I watched mesmerised by all the colourful beauty.

Eventually I realised that it was time to make my way back to the hotel and decided to walk the distance, my KL bearings having improved. The walk took me down into the geographically lower area of the city where the stationary holiday traffic was sending pollution levels up to toxic danger-point. My route continued alongside the coach station where acrid fumes from row upon row of throbbing diesel engines strangled the life out of the dwindling oxygen atoms. With streaming eyes, I entered the hotel just as the light levels fell dramatically. Deciding to slake my thirst before heading back to the Central Station for the airport, with glass poised at lip level, the most almighty tropical storm exploded overhead. The low-light level screeched phosphorescently upwards almost in synch with every ear-splitting crack of thunder. Having downed my beer, without spilling a drop, I gathered up George and somehow squelched my way back to the airport for the Singapore flight with onward connection to Darwin.

My visit had been brief but incredibly interesting and enjoyable; I would certainly consider returning some time in the future. I guess that perhaps a little more research might have paid dividends, but then there is something exciting about just flitting around and watching life buzzing by – isn't that what travel's all about? Perhaps I'm doing myself a disservice, because I did walk miles and I did see a lot. Plus, I was totally comfortable being on my own, although on another occasion I might try to avoid clashing with a public holiday.

Transferring through Singapore for my onward flight to Darwin, the looks on the faces of the Australian passengers were downcast enough to let me know the result of the Rugby World Cup. *Well done, boys*!

Darwin and the Top End

Sunday 23rd November: hello Darwin, where it's five in the morning and raining heavily

Fighting the usual sensations of sleep depravation, I was happily relieved when just one hour after landing, the Holiday Inn allowed me to check-in early at 6am. *Yippee*, as sitting around in a hotel lobby hot, tired and sweaty waiting to be given room keys is a bit of an anticlimax. And talking of sweaty, emerging from the cold of the aircraft hold into the high humidity of Darwin, George too found himself covered in a glistening sheen. The humidity in Kuala Lumpur had been laced with the acrid aroma of car exhausts; this humidity was just pure unadulterated, hair frizzing, damp.

Up to my room to sort myself out, take a cooling shower and flop into bed: my usual arrival routine. A deep dreamless sleep was abruptly interrupted at two in the afternoon as, suddenly wide awake, I knew I had to head outside to explore. No sign of the earlier rain as I emerged from the hotel to walk into the central area of Darwin and then back down and along The Esplanade, where the hotel sits in a prime spot with commanding views across the open expanse of Darwin harbour. Darwin still retained something of an outpost feel and I lapped up the atmosphere.

The Esplanade is a paved walkway which gently dips and

swoops for about 3km as it runs parallel to the harbour. Lush lawns and softly rustling palms create a peaceful environment in which to wander. As I ambled, I came upon Government House, the oldest European building in the Northern Territory. Emerging from the unkempt greenery and standing before this neatly kept historic building, which seemed to float on a sea of manicured green grass, created the sensation of having stepped back in time. Built in the early 1870s, it remains a fine example of mid-Victorian Gothic enlivened by its sparkling white coat of paint. Gothic and confection don't seem natural bedfellows, but that's what it looked like: a pristine Gothic confection. I'm guessing that perhaps the white picket fence was hammered in place to distance the colonial Administrator from the passing public. The building has every reason to stand on its headland position with pride, as it has withstood cyclones, bombs, pest infestations and a rioting rabble. Moving on, I could almost hear the distant chink of porcelain teacups and the swish of ice-cooled gin-slings.

… These were large specimens of the insect family…

Having wandered far enough, I turned and retraced my steps back towards the hotel, where I found my own peaceful sea of green complete with sea-facing bench. Here I sat – just me and a whole bunch of crazy ants busily fossicking in the grass for discarded crumbs – and watched as the sun dipped below the flame-red horizon. Something magical happens at dusk and here, as the light level dimmed, a whispered hush fell over the ebb and flow of the waves and the rustling leaves fell silently still: bliss. Oblivious to the scenic glory and the romanticism of the evening light, the ant activity continued apace. These were large specimens of the insect family so I kept a wary eye on my exposed toes.

Not wishing to change the mood, I reluctantly thought it time to bid farewell to my private retreat. On the way back to the hotel I bought a few snack items from a nearby shop and had a picnic supper in my room before bed. My journal does not record of what I had to drink, but I'm guessing that the hard tack was washed down with a cold beer!

Monday 24th November: a day not to be proud of (I shopped)

So this is Australia's Top End... I last set foot on Darwin dust in approximately 1962 when the airport was still wearing its post-war battle fatigues. It's strange what memories you carry with you over the years: I remember being told that Darwin was the only airport where it was possible to take a shower... this (to me) unheard of luxury was simply a way of providing sweat-drenched travellers with some respite from the Top End's sweat-inducing high humidity.

Life has never been easy in this particular spot on the Australian landscape. Darwin was bombed by the Japanese during their many World War II raids on this strategic area. And the weather has also maintained its own intermittent bombardment. Whether flattened by bombs or flattened by cyclones, Darwin just pulls itself back into shape and life continues.

Sadly, all these historical facts slithered off me and instead my holiday continued less notably than perhaps should have been the case. Most of the day was spent shopping and then at a dressmakers for some alterations; well worth it! I bought a swimming costume, which remained a constant holiday friend for years, until the elastic began to rot and I decided it was time for us to part, before it publicly reached a similar decision. But before I could step into it and head for the water, it needed some tweaking to safely encase my embonpoint.

Joan, a dressmaker working in a tiny shop, was an absolute gem and promised that a little extra strap arrangement would save my blushes. As I worked up a Darwin sweat in her minuscule changing cubicle, wriggling into and out of my new costume, she chatted away telling me all about life in the Top End and visits to Perth in her youth. Living out in the bush, she and her friends would go into the big town for dances on Friday night. There in the dance hall, the men nursed their beers and the women their lambs and baby roos. Carried in the girls' cardigans, the joeys would climb up the woolly sleeves and into the body of the garment emulating the trip up a mum's tum and into the pouch.

Whilst Joan set to with her needle, I walked out to the harbour and watched as a storm built up out at sea. Towering cumuli sat on the horizon, where I guess the weather conditions were rather less calm than here at the water's edge.

At the appointed hour, I was reunited with my new snugly fitting purchase. Thanking Joan for working her magic, I suddenly felt a little sad not be spending more time listening to her tales. Almost feel a tape recorder would have been a worthwhile 'journalistic' investment. In pensive mood, I wandered back to the hotel for an early bed in readiness for an early start the following morning.

Tuesday 25th November: Kakadu National Park

It was just six-fifteen in the morning but I was outside enjoying the early morning calm, ready and waiting for the coach. On cue, it lumbered into view and stopped right beside me, a good guess as I was the only soul visible at that hour. Climbing aboard, was surprised to see that my single ticket had increased the day's tourist total from six to seven: not the high season, obviously. Perhaps it was the early hour, but my fellow travellers did not seem a very cheery bunch, except perhaps for one recent widower who was struggling a little without his much-missed travelling companion. At some point we struck up a conversation and he told me about a luxurious trip that he and his wife had taken to Mandalay sailing up the Irrawaddy River. Made a mental note to add that destination to my still lengthening travel wish-list…

We headed out of town towards the Yellow Water River in Kakadu National Park. The first stop was to allow those who wanted to add a little extra to their day, to do just that. Yes, I was first in line. *And why not?* Recalling my conversation with a concerned Tammie several months ago in the Cook Islands, I nimbly scrambled aboard an even smaller plane than the Aitutaki aircraft. This time I was about to take a trip in a tiny single-engine four-seater Cessna 127. Taking my seat next to the pilot, I settled in my seat with my nose close to the window, ready to enjoy a fifty-five minute scenic flight over the Arnhem Land Escarpment, river and wetlands. The fixed high wings allow an uninterrupted view of what's below, with only the all important strut which 'fixes' the wing to the aircraft body, visible. At one point we turned on a sixpence to take a closer look at a crocodile… or was it just a thrilling manoeuvre to look at a log? I've never yearned to learn to fly, but being buzzed up into the air in one of these tiny manoeuvrable flying machines is an experience I would never want to miss.

The next adventure was on the water, aboard a weather-beaten sailing tub, which floated serenely out to Yellow Water billabong, amid a magical carpet of pink water lilies. The wildlife interest was provided by various colourful and raucous birds and the eyes and tails of slumbering saltie crocodiles: pre-historic sinister beasts. Back on land, we visited the sacred site at Nourlangie Rock to look at the ancient rock art, portraying aspects of Aboriginal mythology and the wildlife which had once roamed the region. The naturally formed shelters within the outcrop have helped to ensure the survival of the art. Amongst the white, yellow and red ochre paintings are images of the now extinct thylacine (Tasmanian tiger) a carnivorous marsupial, with a wolf-like head, tiger-striped body and backward-facing pouch. Thought to have become extinct on mainland Australia several thousand years ago, it survived on the island of Tasmania into the 20th century. The last of this doomed species died in captivity in Hobart, where it is now dustily remembered through the questionable skill of a 1930s taxidermist and the questionable enthusiasm of a contemporary cleaner.

Moving away from Dreamtime, hand and animal paintings, in sombre mood we climbed to the summit of Nourlangie. The awe-inspiring panorama snapped us back to life as we gazed out across the Kakadu wetlands; which whilst now dry would, in a few weeks time, be flooded attracting migrating birds. The day was a really absorbing mix of activities which gradually drew this little group of tourists out of their shells, but even the increased level of chatter could not detract from the feeling of isolation created by the sheer scale of the open landscape. Trying to distinguish possible landmarks, made us realise the navigational skill of the indigenous people who had traversed these lands in their search for food or to join clan members at social and ceremonial gatherings; corroborees. The view across the wetlands is all geography, geology and the impact of weather and not about human intervention. Quite, quite special.

The night was spent at the remote Cooinda Gagudju Lodge; memorable for being built in the shape of a crocodile (best seen from the air). After my usual feast for when I'm hot, tired and sweaty – beer, nuts and lemonade – I went and talked to the sky… it seemed a natural thing to do. I would like to think I was looking at the Pleiades, or Seven Sisters, a star cluster which is important in Aboriginal mythology, but I still haven't really progressed beyond identifying Orion and his belt.

Totally contented, I returned to my little room where I slept soundly, happy in the knowledge that my new hiking boots were a success. Climbing sure-footed over rocky terrain, I felt like a gecko... I could stick to anything in my boots; they were an excellent purchase.

Wednesday 26th November: the sound of the didgeridoo

Today our small party visited the Aboriginal paintings at Ubirr rock to again gaze upon ancient art forms. As before, the art occurs within the natural shelters of a rocky outcrop, this time located on the edge of the Nadab floodplain. Here it seems as if the depictions of the creation ancestors are of a more aquatic nature: barramundi, catfish, mullet and turtles swim along the surfaces. I think somewhere in their midst a thylacine prowls, but I didn't see him. Admittedly, historically the Aboriginal people would retouch paintings to keep the images vibrant and viable as didactic tools, so it was difficult distinguishing art that was several thousand years old from art of a few centuries in age. Either way, they exuded an air of mysticism. To see the art you have to climb, and the reward is two-fold – the art and the panoramic views across the floodplain and escarpments (the trainers of my last trip have been usurped by my walking boots).

The vastness of the views was completely breathtaking. At the site a local Aboriginal guide gave a spell-binding talk explaining the culture and mythology of his people, plus he played the didgeridoo fabulously. I hadn't appreciated the range of sounds that could be achieved on this seemingly simple wind instrument nor had I given any thought to the skill required in breathing in and blowing out at the same time to achieve those sounds. The didgeridoo playing at Uluru had been good, but this was better: quite wonderful. As I discovered at Uluru, to hear the didgeridoo being played in its natural home is really rather special.

After the exertion of rock climbing, it was off to Guluyambi to embark upon a cruise on the East Alligator River. The relaxation didn't last long as we drifted up to the Arnhem Land shore of the river where, on land, we had a practical lesson in fire-making. Sadly, I didn't progress past the theory. But we weren't all bad students as one in our party managed to get some 'amber fire' going with relative ease, which made me wonder why Ray Mears always makes such a big thing about lighting a fire. Seeing the blisters on the palm of my hand later in the day, perhaps I was being a bit churlish towards Ray's skills. The land upon which this fire-making activity was taking place can only be accessed with permission from the traditional owners, the Yolngu people. I might have been in Arnhem Land for a few minutes, but I did feel it was a privilege to be there.

In the afternoon we popped in to the Bowali Creek Visitor Centre, which was a bit ditto if you've been to the centre at Uluru. Just feel the information could be imparted a little more imaginatively... especially when the human guides are so brilliant at sharing their oral culture. The route back to Darwin took us to another visitor centre, the Window on the Wetlands Visitor Centre, which sits atop Beatrice Hill, one of the highest points on the Adelaide River floodplain. The information leaflet drew my attention to the design of the building. Glancing up, the upswept roofline did indeed appear fluid as it represents the wings of a dancing brolga. These large Australian cranes dance as part of their mating ritual; singly, in pairs or in social groups. They also gaily toss grass skywards as part of their ritual, creating an image of being the party animals of the bird-world.

Sadly these (and other) spectacular wetland birds were predictably noticeable by their absence, but it must be a twitchers' haven at the right time of the year. However, Mother Nature generously provided an alternative spectacular sight, standing with a glass of wine in my hand and nibbles at my elbow, I watched in total fascination as (once again) storm clouds of epic proportion gathered away in the distance, over Darwin.

Back at the hotel, reflecting upon all I had seen and done, I decided that my trip to Kakadu National Park had indeed been 'awesome'. I felt a long way from anywhere and enjoyed the experience so much, that I would really like to return. However, next time I'd opt for the wet season, to have a go at bird watching and hopefully witness the courtship rituals of the dancing brolgas. The best time for bird-watching is less challengingly referred to as the 'green season', covering the months from December to March: I was just on the cusp.

Thursday 27th November: another terrific day

Today I'm off to the Katherine River, but only after what turned out to be a very emotional first stop at the Adelaide River War Cemetery. The cemetery, established in 1942, is a memorial to the 430 plus service personnel who lost their lives during the sixty-four Japanese air raids on Darwin. The cemetery also contains the Northern Territory Memorial which commemorates the lives of those service personnel who have no known grave.

Set on the banks of the Adelaide River, the grounds are especially beautiful with lush lawns and colourful flower gardens. Against this serene backdrop the epitaphs are difficult to read without shedding a tear. A peacock family manages to soften the solemnity of the surroundings and their antics were described to us. Father, having done what nature requires him to do, divorces himself from family matters. Harassed mother tries to sit on her new clutch of eggs, but jealous juvenile son won't let her. So Mum has to practice ways of getting him physically drawn away from the eggs and occupied, so that she can sneak back to the cooling clutch. The two men who look after the cemetery, and who told us about the dynamics of the peacock family, obviously do so with love and reverence. An early lunch at the Adelaide River Inn was a bit of a shift in mood as, on the bar, stands 'Charlie' the stuffed water buffalo and local (deceased) resident made famous for his role in the movie, *Crocodile Dundee*. He is/was a big chap!

The afternoon was total bliss as we ventured into the Nitmiluk National Park for a trip down the Katherine River through two of the thirteen deep-sided sandstone gorges. Rapids and waterfalls complete this geological wonder. Mooring up we burnt a few beer-fuelled calories with a now familiar walk and scramble over rock-strewn land between the two gorges for a look at some more Aboriginal rock paintings. By now my brain was struggling, I had so enjoyed looking at the previous paintings, but art was now losing out to my eagerness to be back in the water. Consequently, my attention was not quite as it should have been as I was mentally on my way back to the boat, before the art had even been reached.

Culture dispensed with, we all trotted back to the boat in double-quick time – we knew what was next on the agenda and were impatient to get going. The watery meander home took us via Edith Falls for a swim in the paperbark and pandanus fringed fresh-water pool. The falls were in subdued mode awaiting the arrival of the rains which would convert the lazy trickle into a raging torrent. It didn't matter one jot as swimming and floating in the cool clear water was delicious. With grateful thanks to Joan, I remained safely in place within my new swimming costume as I drifted on my back looking up into a clear blue Australian sky. Much as I love sea swimming, the fresh-water version is a rare treat. When the conditions are right (warm) I would certainly cast off into the English Channel, but I don't find much appeal in squelching through the cold mud of an English riverbed or pond.

Huh, mud is nothing. It was only after this dreamy interlude that I learnt that freshwater crocodiles also enjoy drifting in the cool water of the Katherine River. On cue, a junior version, an exact replica of an adult in miniature, had wriggled to the water's edge where it remained inert as if posing just for us. I silently thanked him for his magical timing. These reptiles are harmless to humans, unlike their saltie cousins who enter the pool when the water levels rise during the wet season. Just in case anyone feels the macho need to gamble with their lives, there are signs reminding the foolhardy that swimming is banned in the wet season. I didn't ask, but when the waters recede, do the salties recede with it… or do the park rangers give these prehistoric reptiles a gentle nudge… or were interlopers still hiding log-like under the pandanus as I swam by? If I swam up against a crocodile, would I hang around to identify its genus? Freshwater or saltie… I'd be out in a flash.

… On cue…a junior version wriggled to the water's edge

These sharp-toothed thoughts did not spoil my appetite. To round off an already idyllic day, we stopped for a barramundi and mash supper: *yum*! I couldn't have conjured up a more delicious ending to my Kakadu National Park experience.

Friday 28th November: a last day in the fascinating Top End

Awoke this morning feeling a little sad that this part of my journey was coming to an end, it was as if I wasn't ready to move on but wanted instead to retrace my steps and see more of the Northern Territory. Once again I felt that visceral tug which had caught me off kilter at Uluru. Packing George I wondered how to fill the few hours between checking out of the hotel and checking in for the flight to Perth. Having relinquished my room key, not sure how this came about, but one of the 'lads' from the hotel drove me down to the quayside where I had a fresh orange juice. Sitting in splendid isolation I realised that all around me the neighbouring cafes and shops seemed to be reflecting my mood – they had taken on that sad 'closed' out of season look. As soon as the cyclones are due, the itinerant tourist-trade-staff begin to drift away in search of work in a more equitable climate.

Sipping my drink, I mused upon how much I had warmed to Darwin and the people I had met. It is an ethnically diverse community and on arrival in Darwin I had had no idea of the important role undertaken by the immigrant Chinese population in the town's development and frequent reconstruction. Since the European settlement, Darwin has been flattened four times and after each wave of devastation it was the Chinese community who helped ensure, by dint of their hard work, that a new Darwin rose phoenix-like from the metaphorical and literal ashes.

Bidding a fond farewell to the harbour I caught a shuttle bus back into town where it was so hot, I downed another orange juice. Taking a final amble through the town, I whispered a silent farewell to the Aboriginal family sitting in the shade of an ancient tree, to Joan and the shopkeepers who had been so chatty and charming and to Darwin itself. Somehow I sensed that in a few years, the city would have grown and transformed itself. My visit was on the cusp of that change and I'm glad I saw it before it became too slick. I then sauntered back to the hotel to board the airport shuttle bus. The delayed flight finally got me into Perth at 5pm where I was just in time to catch another shuttle bus, this time to my slightly out of town accommodation, Sullivans Hotel.

Sullivans is a welcoming family-run establishment situated on Mounts Bay Road and nestled beneath King's Park. Struggling up the four steps from the car park into the reception area brought back memories of diving headlong onto the pavement in Sydney... perhaps the steps are a bit steep? Not sure why, but they did present George and me with a challenge. As I fought to get a grip, I became aware of several jaw-grinding diners silently watching me through the plate glass dining room window: it was hard not to giggle. The window protrudes alongside the steps and into the car park, so comings and goings provide diners with unscheduled entertainment. However, when in the dining room, the watchers become the watched as a parked row of V8 engines appears to be looking up hungrily at the hotel guests. Hints of Stephen King's *Christine* perhaps?

Step-challenge completed, I made my way towards the discreetly head-bowed receptionist and in no time at all was immersed in a happy evening re-arranging the contents of George and attending to my laundry. There's nothing like the hum of the washing machine to snap me out of nostalgic reveries! On this occasion the laundry room was located close to the hotel's tiny swimming pool and garden, where I discovered it was relaxing to sit in the evening with a good book, whilst waiting for the machine to go through its cool wash cycle.

As this was my second visit to Perth, it really did feel like home.

Perth: Welcome Back

Saturday 29th November: a day of culture

I awoke to the sounds of the city – a combination of the constant flow of traffic, strangely heading out of town, and the raucous racket of the crow community. If I stay in Australia too long, I might miss the gentle dawn chorus of England.

Hungry, as ever, it was off to the infamous dining room to tuck into the more than adequate 'continental'. The waiter was mortified by my abstemiousness (if only he knew). It seemed that the Trailfinders rate included the full cooked works, and he tried every which way to make me change my mind. This is probably the only occasion on my travels when I've actually turned down an offer of food. Whilst munching through my granola, I became aware of an odd one-sided conversation taking place behind me. Someone was asking questions, pausing and then commenting on what must have been the replies…but I couldn't hear them. The companion must have had a tiny voice because we are only inches away from one another. As I got up to go I discovered that the one-sided conversation was indeed just that, one-sided. A lone chap was chatting to himself. Oh dear, I have a sneaking suspicion that I might be guilty, in a more subtle fashion, of doing the same thing. Let that be a warning.

Map in hand, I walked in to Perth, approximately fifteen minutes away, and down to the Swan River and over on the ferry to south Perth where I visited the Art Gallery of Western Australia which contains an eclectic and fascinating mix of artefacts in all media, including installations. I stood transfixed before a small painting by the Australian artist Frederick McCubbin entitled, *Down on His Luck* (1889). It depicts an out of work swagman sitting slumped on a fallen log; here were two fallen souls. The weight of the man's despair is palpable and, unsurprisingly, this allegorical image has remained seared on my brain… where I expect it will stay forever more.

Continuing the theme of despair (only a tenuous link) the new build section of the art gallery connects to a 19th-century building which once housed the Perth Police Courts. The collection continues into this space and adorns walls which would once have witnessed sights considerably different to the sights of wandering tourists. The two holding cells seemed to chime guilty before the prisoner had covered the short walk to the courtroom where the dock was plain and austere (for the sinner) whilst the witness stand was carved and ornate (for the sinned upon).

After a long session of culture, I wandered and ambled and absorbed Perth life. I went down to the Swan Bells again, but felt no desire to further my skills as a campanologist instead I had a cup of coffee by the water. I then went in search of the old mint, but gave up a road intersection too early, as I later realised. And so decided that having walked about as far away from my hotel as was possible, whilst remaining within the city limits, it was time to turn around and head for home.

Close to the hotel I dropped into a bottle shop and bought a bottle of beer and borrowed a bottle opener. The cool drink refreshed me as I set about a stint at the keyboard sending emails home. Another very satisfying day had been ticked off the calendar.

Sunday 30th November: black swans on the Swan River

First task was to return the bottle opener before I then climbed Jacobs Ladder, a steep pathway just behind the hotel, to King's Park where I wiled away several pleasant hours. Appropriately, the tree top walk provides you with a birds-eye panoramic view of Perth and the Swan River, on which floated the first black swans that I had seen in Western Australia. These elegant birds posed the same conundrum as the robins in New Zealand: how can a southern hemisphere bird seem so like its northern hemisphere cousin? Some more avian evolutionary research is needed.

Facing away from the water, the main approach to the park runs along Fraser Avenue, which is lined with handsome white-barked lemon-scented gums. These majestic trees provide a guard of honour leading to another of Australia's spectacular parks. Here pathways meander up and down gentle slopes, water burbles from streams to ponds, children cartwheel on springy grass, and trees of every description provide both shade and colour. On a branch of a sparsely leafed specimen, a kookaburra obligingly cackled. Hooray! Another native 'must see' seen. Although technically in the wild, he was obviously used to strolling visitors, so he sat quietly, now mute, whilst I inspected him from all angles. Yes, there was no mistaking the fact that he was a member of the kingfisher family. He might be the national bird emblem of New South Wales, but he looked very at home in Western Australia. My Australian wildlife tally was finally on the increase.

Leaving King's Park – eventually – I looped my way around and back into town where I raided a hole in the wall for 300 dollars. This amount was rather more than I usually withdraw, but tomorrow I would be on the road again heading into the unknown, so this was my insurance. I spent a small portion of the money on a book, one that I had heard of but had never read: *We of the Never Never*. Reading it after my visits to the Top End and the Red Centre and now whilst travelling to the gold fields and the Wheatbelt region was entirely appropriate, as these are all areas of the 'never never', the outback. Written in 1902 by Jeannie Gunn, the book is a memoir of an eventful year spent with her husband on a remote cattle station in the Northern Territory just 300 miles south of Darwin. Jeannie arrived as a bride and left as a widow, her husband having died from malarial dysentery. Many of the incidents she described are horrific as they detail the battle between settlers and the indigenous people who were being starved off their ancestral land. But she was also meticulous at portraying life in a harsh and unforgiving climate – her writing voice is measured and calm whereas mine, under similar circumstances, would have come across as being high-pitched and increasingly hysterical.

My own short odyssey would take me across remote regions where the hardships that became Jeannie's way of life would be familiar to the families who lived and worked there today. My planned route was to head east to Kalgoorlie-Boulder, south to the coast at Esperance and then back to Perth along the more densely populated coast via the Margaret River region. For part of the journey I would be out in the back of beyond: the 'never never'. That's why I needed the money! I hadn't booked hotels or motels, instead opting for lady luck to join George as my travelling companions.

It was early to bed that night, I had a long way to travel tomorrow. But first I had to read a few of Jeannie's chapters...

Heading east from Perth

Monday 1st December: let the next road adventure begin

Hooray! A bright and sunny day and the open roads beckon. Wandered around to Avis to pick up my Astra only to find that it had transmogrified into a Holden V6 Commodore, very nice too in its shiny tomato red livery. I'm sure if I booked a small car expecting an upgrade, the upgrade would never happen. But to date my unexpected success rate has been 100 percent.

Once again George had room to waltz and tango around in the boot. Confident that I could navigate east, I headed out of town for York. First problem – why do roads which appear straight on the map in reality have T junctions with unknown destinations signposted rather than somewhere you want to go? Drove through a 'drive-thru' bottle shop for the car park at the rear where I turned the map upside down and every which way and decided that the right fork was probably what I wanted. Hallelujah… it was. By lunchtime I had passed through Mundaring (the Aboriginal name for a high place on a high place) and reached the outskirts of York, no wait it was York… just one slightly dusty road with a few tiny residential areas clustered off and around. So who had built York and why? Turning to the well-thumbed pages of my guide book, I note that…

In 1830 European settlers from the Swan River Colony explored the country east of the Darling Range and were delighted to find the Avon Valley [where] land was grabbed eagerly and the district has been a successful agricultural region ever since. Situated by the Avon River, York experienced a short boom in the 1890s when gold was discovered in the east of the state. At that time York was the easternmost rail terminus and the last source of fresh water but was soon passed by when both water and rail reached Kalgoorlie.[5]

Excuse the slight digression, as I have just read 'water' and found the following information relevant as the engineering feat that was CY O'Connor's water pipeline would accompany me along stretches of my drive. The 330-mile pipeline was constructed at the end of the 19th century to take water from Perth to the goldfields at Kalgoorlie and is still in use today, providing water to towns along the route before reaching its destination. Water was sourced by damming the Helena River, Perth and creating storage in the Mount Charlotte Reservoir, Kalgoorlie. The concrete pipe sits above ground where its simplicity belies the life-giving properties of its contents. Maybe as an engineering project it's not as awe inspiring as some, but it scores highly for its utility. And it sort of kept me company as I clocked up the miles.

Back in York, lunch was enjoyed in splendid isolation in the courtyard of the Settlers Inn, a delightful late 19th-century building adorned with some wonderfully evocative sepia photographs. My lunch spot was not the only building of note along this stretch of road. Historically, when the town lost its rail status to nearby Northam, which became the major rail junction to the goldfields, it also lost the need for urban expansion. Consequently, the town's original buildings remained peacefully unspoilt. My lunch-time musings drifted back to the people in the photographs. Close to York lies the town of Beverley, so I wondered if these early settlers had come from Yorkshire. Possibly no, as not too far away Kelmscott managed to scotch that theory. English spellings of indigenous place-names co-exist alongside settler developed and named towns, providing an historical cultural mix.

After my thoughtful lunch, I visited the Old Courthouse and Gaol, a small museum complex which was well preserved and well presented and once again provided evidence of the terrible treatment meted out against the hapless and bewildered Aboriginal people. But here was further evidence of the cultural mix, as it wasn't only the indigenous population which felt the might of the law. York, the first developed inland town in Western Australia, also had unruly members of the white settler community and convicts to contend with. Therefore, a strong police presence was needed. Those in custody were chained together with the chains attached to heavy metal collars, still visible today. All very grim and it did generate an involuntary *ugh* shudder.

Seeking a change of tempo, I made my way towards York's best known attraction, its Motor Museum. I parted with a tiny entrance fee, turned the corner and stood looking at an incredible line-up of approximately 150 vintage and classic cars, most of which were said to be in working order. The vehicles represented the 'evolution of motor transport', and had been amassed by the museum's founder, Peter Briggs. Here were examples of mechanical innovation from the earliest eras of the combustion engine through to their more modern successors. In addition to cars I had never heard of, such as the 1919 Australian Six Tourer ('Made in Australia, by Australians for Australia') there were several old friends, such as an evocative MGTC.

Reading the museum blurb, I discovered that the owner's mother had raced them, which caused an *aah* moment as I had learnt to drive in one. It was thanks to the leakiness of the TC that for years after I would involuntarily lift my legs when driving through puddles, a reflex that worked better as a passenger than driver. HKO 445... *whatever happened to you?* More nostalgia, this time in the sensuous curvy shape of an MGA, the car which followed the TC in my life and has never been forgotten: I'm not sure that I ever got the distance between steering wheel and front bumper quite right, but it was such fun to drive. Next in my life came the MGB, but so did babies, and the sporty MG had to give way to a sensible Renault 5. Not quite the same.

As I wandered amongst this intriguing (but slightly dusty) collection of cars, 'Peter' came up to me and we began to chat, correction, I listened. Re-reading what follows, I seem to have forgotten the car aspect of anything Peter said and written about his personal life. He said that he was married to Swiss-born Ursula, who wasn't wildly keen on remote York as she kept asking him why he wasn't back with her, rather than with these 'dusty' (my insertion) cars. Yesterday he had won the veteran Australian fencing championship... he was born in Portsmouth... went to Kings School, Canterbury... played Benenden (I might have raised my eyebrows as I thought this an all girls school, but perhaps that was the point)... has a son also named Peter (although I think Piers might be the correct spelling)... misses the English sense of humour... and on and on he charmingly went! I was in the museum much longer than intended (and not just listening but also looking) and I found the whole experience jaw-droppingly fascinating. I can now add Motor Museums to my list of things done well in Australia, in addition to botanical gardens and art galleries.

For years after this encounter I assumed that I had been talking to Peter Briggs, founder and ex-racing driver, but it was only when I picked up a copy of *The Western Australian* newspaper dated 15th March 2016 that I realised I had been listening to Peter Harbin, curator and ex-racing driver. It was with sadness that I read that Peter Harbin had recently died. Here was confirmation of his life-long passions of cars and fencing and a description of how from 1999 he had been the curator of the York Motor Museum. In an endeavour to breathe life into the cars, Peter had organised events to get them out onto the streets of York (perhaps I'd been looking at outback dust on their bonnets). The obituary concluded with: 'here was an English endearing eccentric on the fringes of the outback'.

My brain is still struggling to come to terms with the fact that in Albany, Western Australia, in March 2016, I had stopped for a cup of coffee and randomly selected this one newspaper from a pile of reading material. I feel very privileged to have met Peter and appreciate that his enthusiasm for anything associated with the whiff of Castrol GTX and burning rubber, made him an ideal guardian of those magnificent historic cars: *requiescat in pace*.

But back in 2003, what could so easily have felt like my release from the above chatter was in fact a departure made out of necessity. I had yet to find a room for the night and crossed the road to find Peter's recommendation, The Imperial. And there on Avon Terrace it stood, in all its Victorian ironwork glory, with a pub downstairs and rooms around the upstairs balcony. The room rate was 70 dollars, including food: an absolute bargain. The 19th-century exterior was mirrored in its 19th-century interior, the bedroom not much more than a metal bed in a broom cupboard, and no en suite just a short hike over creaky floorboards to the ladies bathroom. Kevin, the proprietor, wanted me to have the pick of the rooms, but as the curtains were falling down in all the rooms he showed me, there seemed to be no particular hierarchical merit to attract me, so chose what I thought was the lightest and airiest. Fortunately I had a small safety pin about my person and it did a grand job of preserving my nighttime modesty as it fought to hold the curtains both up and together. However, I was at a loss as to how to solve the problem of no bedroom key... so slept with one eye open and George standing guard by the door.

Undeterred by the air of decrepitude, I sat outside for my inclusive curry supper, getting bitten to blazes. The one and only staff member kept calling me "M'lady" which made me want to say, "But my name's not Penelope" as images of *Thunderbirds* circa the 1960s kept flashing before my eyes. I wasn't sure if the now mentally christened 'Parker' was p**s-taking... would probably guess that he was... although he did seem quite chirpy in the way that he addressed his one and only customer of the evening. He did an excellent selling job on the feast he was about to serve, announcing that it would consist of ten courses.

"Wow," said an amazed I.

"Yes," said a cheery he. "Bread, butter, vegemite, rice, sauce, meat..." went the list.

'Very droll, Parker,' thought Lady P.

All in all it was a surprisingly happy and satisfying stay – just had to ignore the layers of (more) dust and the fact that the lace cover on the dark oak 1930s dressing table was an off-cut of carpet anti-slip stuff. For all my concerns about a lack of key, I slept soundly, obviously satisfied that delegating security to an inert suitcase was a normal thing to do.

Kevin had said that breakfast would be available from eight. With a busy day ahead, I rose early, showered in a facility reminiscent (visually and odour-wise) of a girls' hockey club changing room and at eight-fifteen ventured downstairs... it was like the *Marie Celeste*. With no sign of food, not even a packet of cereal, I gathered up my belongings and crept out into the day, the clock by now registering two minutes past nine as I exited to the sound of silence. Later I discovered a voicemail message from Kevin (in York) asking me to call him, which I didn't, as he was probably asking me to "make breakfast if you're first up"... I hope it was nothing serious and to this day I don't know why I didn't return his call. This omission will haunt me (I'm certain I paid my bill) as in 2014 I was saddened to read that the hotel had closed 'permanently'. To be honest, I was more than a little surprised that it had limped along for so long. Could it be that Kevin is now a distant memory in a few people's minds? A minute's silence is needed here.

Oh dear, there is a further post-script. I had found my stay in York so endearing that I revisited in 2016, hoping that in the intervening two years the hotel had been snapped up and new life breathed into its iron-work glory. Alas, the permanent as in closed 'permanently' was still holding fast. It's a really beautiful building which deserves to be preserved. *Any takers*?

Tuesday 2nd December: off into the wilds

Having bid a nostalgic farewell to a slumbering York, I headed south driving out through Beverley to the Wheatbelt towns of Brookton and Corrigin where I stopped for a snack. Corrigin is no oil painting, it's tiny, flat and utilitarian but the dog cemetery signifies its soft underbelly. Pulling over, I got out and began wandering amongst an assortment of doggy graves, here lying side-by-side were pampered pooches and working hounds all remembered with great affection, as the lines of verse and assortment of well-chewed toys eloquently showed. Keeping guard over these memorials to man's best friend, sat a very fine statue of a proud working dog. His upright alert countenance signified Corrigan's claim to fame: it is the 'home of the dog in the ute'. Once upon a time all utility vehicles had a utility dog slipping and sliding about, or sometimes tethered, in the open back. Now in these days of health and safety dogs are more commonly seen sitting inside the cab staring out through the windscreen, wistfully remembering the whoosh of the wind in their ears and the nostril-flaring intoxication of passing heady scents: the stuff of canine dreams.

After this doggy interlude, I was drawn to a large agricultural building which housed a supermarket, I wandered inside in search of water and a snack and realised that this was truly a 'one stop shop', as it sold everything for the pastoralist and the housewife but it looked as if neither had passed through the doorway in many a decade. Everything appeared to be old and dusty and certainly end-of-line and the musty mints I bought reinforced my impression. On reflection, perhaps I'm a bit slow on registering my surroundings, as possibly the parched landscape of the agricultural area through which I was driving had something to do with the layers of dust I kept encountering...

Having shopped, I then pushed open a creaky door to the Café Papier Mâché... a little bit surreal. In a barn-like space I gazed upon some bits of art paper and twiddly things for making decorations, one or two objet d'art and a really eclectic assortment of tables and chairs plus a huge table laden with paper, crayons, etc, to occupy the younger coffee consumer. Amid this creative vortex, I sat and enjoyed a homemade Florentine and mocha for my breakfast and was enchanted by the slip of a girl who, seemingly, managed the venture. As Corrigin is 235km from Perth, I guess it's important to work in ways that will keep the community vibrant and cohesive. I left hoping that the coffee shop would prosper... but it was a really incongruous find in the middle of a very serious farming community. I'm sure everyone enjoys some downtime with a cup of coffee and company, but I wasn't really sure about the papier-mâché aspect. Checking on-line twelve years later, it looks like the venture may have succeeded under a rebranding as the Mallee Tree Café and Gallery with an emphasis on selling furniture and ornaments carved from the wood of the mallee tree (a multi-stemmed eucalypt). I hope the young girl who served me is still the driving force behind the project.

Revived by the sugar-rush of my breakfast, I continued

my journey through the wheat fields of Western Australia – yesterday, today, tomorrow – vast, vast, vast. Huge machinery was busily employed bringing in the harvest, the air of urgency tangible as storms were predicted. Picked up *Country Hour* on the radio and prepared to settle back and listen to an hour of Tammy Wynette – instead it was all about goat mortalities during transport, the plight of dairy farmers and the optimism of wheat farmers – which political commentators felt was misplaced. The transmission also covered issues such as the closure of local hospitals, disaffected youth and internal squabbling within the political parties: home from home, really.

Arrived at Hyden about oneish and refuelled, bought more water and then drove round to the Wave Rock Motel to check in. Refreshed and revived, I headed out again in the direction of my goal for the day: Wave Rock. Wow. The name is no mere whimsical fancy. The granite formation is an inviting 15 metres high and 110 metres long, and I didn't look overly hard for sign posts respectfully asking tourists not to climb the rock, so up to the top I went. And what views greeted me. Both peering down over the edge of the splendidly uniform curl and gazing out across an area pitted with salt lakes and dotted with scrubby bush, either way it was hauntingly majestic. By now I should be used to seeing horizons of global proportions, but once again a panoramic view of not a lot was awe inspiring. In the distance, the only blip on the horizon was the rock formation, The Humps, where Mulka's Cave can be found with its mystical hand imprints. An Aboriginal legend tells how the largest and highest prints belong to Mulka, a giant whose cross-eyes prevented him from hunting with a spear… so he caught and ate children. Perhaps that's the magic. You look at nothing, but 'nothing' hides a whole universe… such as child-eating giants.

Investigating my smooth rocky surroundings, there in a sheltered hollow grew a lone sandalwood tree, a gnarled reminder of the days when these precious trees were plentiful

– the days before settlers cut them down. I'm not an arboreal expert, the tree was labelled. Time to retreat and as the climb up had been far from arduous I thought the descent would be likewise. Silly me, my 'stick to anything' shoes suddenly slipped into ice-skating mode. Having climbed up feeling tall, nimble and lithe I descended hunched, crab-like and doddery – feeling ever more pitiful as words of encouragement were wafted in my direction by a dad whose brood of small children scooted around my ankles fearlessly. As did a number of agile lizards, which obviously thought this lumbering lady was no threat. Having made it safely to the bottom, a cool drink was in order before my next escapade. Sipping my drink, I decided that it was probably just as well I hadn't climbed Uluru. Had I done so, my name would probably have been added to one of those chilling plaques.

Refreshed, I walked the 1.5km circuit to see the Hippo's Yawn rock and oddly the few people who had been on Wave Rock just seemed to evaporate and I was on my own and a bit spookily on my own, with not even a scuttling lizard for company. I like to think that I didn't keep looking over my shoulder, but I might have done so once or twice. The track led through fairly dense scrub, which I clomped across, over and under in double-quick time. Emerging from the thicket (had I been on the right track?) I stood before a yawning hippo. It didn't require any stretch of the imagination to understand how this gaping void in the granite had acquired its name. Like its oceanic granite cousin, it couldn't have been called anything else, as here was the head of a larger than life yawning hippo. I would like to have stood in its gaping maw for a true touristy photo, but there was nobody around to do the honours for me. So I just stood and pretended.

My circumnavigation of the route had not been so speedy that I failed to notice the last remaining petals of the spring flowers, there were just enough blown blooms to make me appreciate how dramatically different the scrub must look when the flowers are at their colourful best. As ever, I'm just a bit too early or a bit too late for nature's most flamboyant moments. Tantalisingly, the hot air still carried a potpourri hay-like whiff.

Today's adventure had been both stunningly captivating and hotly sweaty, so back to the motel I went where I de-bugged the windscreen, said goodnight to the Commodore and retreated to my room where I settled down to watch (why?) *Extreme Makeovers...* and I mean extreme. Peering through splayed fingers, I squeaked *ouch* each time a new procedure was embarked upon. Still, the end results seemed incredible... it's amazing what a few nips and tucks can do to knock back the years. All the same, I will learn to live in harmony with my excess adipose tissue.

Drifting off to sleep after my arduous day, I was suddenly back in the land of the living and wide awake: the downside of low-cost accommodation is that the soundproofing is usually non-existent. The German couple in the room next to mine talked and talked and talked...

Wednesday 3rd December: just me and PC Coates

Breakfast was a too sweet Special K bar but at least I was on the road by eight forty-five. What a fabulous drive! The road was a mix of single and double track which sliced its way through wonderful scenery and then zigzagged across country on a road which didn't appear on my map but which the hotel receptionist had told me, with absolute confidence, would be the best route to my destination: Kalgoorlie.

Bowling along with not much going my way, just the occasional dust-devil-creating road train bearing down on me on its way to Perth and the odd anachronistic ute with de rigueur upright dog in the back staring intently at the receding skyline whilst maintaining impeccable balance. On and off the sandy/gravelly edges I went, avoiding dust-swirling road trains and wondering if the Commodore was equally enjoying this freedom of the open road. At Merredin I hit the Great Eastern Highway. The town sits in the central Wheatbelt at a point roughly midway between Perth and Kalgoorlie. I drove through Merredin, unaware that a visit to the Railway Museum might have been a good idea and opted, instead, to head for a coffee stop at Southern Cross, a name which sounded both romantic and patriotic, little dreaming of how much in need of the coffee I would be by then.

Somewhere after Merredin near the town of Walgoolan, an Aboriginal name meaning a place where the short bushes grow, and before Southern Cross, coming over an incline and heading down into a long deserted straight set in a landscape peppered with 'short bushes' I noticed a car in the distance with lights on the roof... he'd appeared out of nowhere and was driving towards me. By the time I had hit the brake pedal, said lights were lit up just like a sparkly Christmas tree. Pulling over I had no option but to let down the window and smile at the unsmiling face of PC Coates.

"How fast do you think you were going?" he asked sternly.

Somehow, with his trendy shades and pink lip sun screen, I couldn't get as twitchy as undoubtedly I would have done had he been a hard-nosed representative of the traffic cop division. Unfortunately I didn't endear myself to PC Coates by uttering something totally inane as I handed over my licence. I suffered a further indignity and a blush of embarrassment when a lorry I had whizzed past several kilometers back trundled by with a toothy "tee hee" from driver and mate. Perhaps at this point I gave an involuntary nervous smirk, because a short lecture followed on the seriousness of my felony and ended with, "I suggest you drive a little more slowly in future, ma'am."

Sadly... my traffic cop charm offensive had fallen flat...

Lecture over, I received a virtual three points on my licence because it wasn't Australian and an actual 150 dollar fine to be paid in Kalgoorlie, without fail or be banned from driving in Western Australia for ever more. Blinking my contrition, I was then free to go.

I had been cruising at 134kph in a 110 (national) limit. Was the relief of only a 150 dollar fine obvious on my face, I wonder? Yes, I know speeding can be dangerous but there are times when the conditions just invite a little play... but perhaps someone was watching over me bringing me back into check before greater damage was done. Continuing onwards my strictly adhered to 110kph did seem a bit of a dawdle. And as I pottered along, I ruminated a little sadly on the fact that my traffic cop charm offensive had fallen totally flat. Middle age brings both benefits and detractions... and I'm probably guilty of sexist thoughts.

Back on track, I remembered my scheduled 'revive, survive' stop at Southern Cross where I pulled into the service station, wailing, "I want a sausage sandwich," which swiftly arrived, all hot and delicious, to be washed down with a comforting mug of tea. Duly revived, I continued sedately on my way to Kalgoorlie.

The urban sprawl of this mining town reached out to greet me in a non-too welcoming manner. Making a snap decision, I rejected the ply-wood motels and opted for a couple of nights of splendour at the Australian right slap bang on central

Hannan Street. Well, it seemed like a good idea. The room was very small with nowhere to put George other than under the basin in the bijou bathroom – could be worse. A quick spit and polish later, I sauntered out for my usual bearings getting recce, dropped off more film to be developed and then sought out the Post Office to pay my speeding fine. This handsome building with its impressive solid clock tower is the main subject for the few postcards which exist of Kalgoorlie-Boulder (in 1989 these two mining towns amalgamated). Crossing the threshold was to journey back in time. The friendly staff stood behind a handsome highly polished wooden counter, free from security glass, tut-tutting over PC Coates' inhospitable act of levying a fine. Cheered by their good humour, I enjoyed a mug of green tea and an apricot biscuit in the café next door.

Having perused my guide book, I set off to find the brothel – which wasn't quite what I had in mind and perhaps accounted for the hotel receptionist's raised eyebrows when I asked for directions. I thought I was about to take an historical look at an important Victorian service, but no, the red light district is current and thriving. One house does have tours three times daily but the focus is more on the 21st-century trade rather than the 19th-century activities. There has been talk about opening a brothel museum but the good matrons of the region keep putting their collective foot down: shame, as I guess it would be very interesting. Anyway, I had walked miles expecting to find one of the old tin 'starting boxes' – so called because the row of tin brothel rooms looked like the starting stalls at the nearby racetrack – but in their place was a smart new brick building: Langtrees Brothel. The next tour was at 6pm and as it was only four-thirty decided to amble back into town to see what the information office had to offer. Here I was in gold-fever town, so the heritage and mine tour for the next morning seemed ideal.

I rounded off my rather weird day with half a pint of Murphy's in the Tart 'n' Miner pub where the décor was decidedly tartan, so a bit of a play on words. *H'mm*, very funny. Back to the hotel for a quick change and then off to Monty's a couple of streets away for a hearty steak and egg supper. Finally, after a long day, it was back again to my tiny room to catch up on writing and an early night in readiness for tomorrow's trip.

Then – No! Just after midnight I awoke to the sound of a brawl. No, it was a telly blaring in the next room, the changing music gave the game away, and then a loud conversation erupted in the corridor outside my door. The noise continued until one forty-five when I donned my sexy pink cover-up, brushed my hair, and strode out to ask, "Please could you continue your conversation elsewhere?" A few belligerent replies later and peace finally descended until 6am when they were back yakking in the corridor again. I got up early, had breakfast and checked out saying that one night was quite enough. Thank you very much.

Thursday 4th December: a date with 'Super Pit'

With my tour booked for 9.30am, I retrieved the car from the hotel garage, manoeuvred it out from its allotted space, into a tiny alleyway and slowly emerged into the main road. Drove around a block or two and found the Mercure Plaza and checked in to a top of the range king-size room – apparently all they had left, but at least the price included breakfast. Again manoeuvred my car into its allotted space and set off for my trip.

First stop was the main hub for the Royal Flying Doctor Service (RFDS) which was fairly interesting, when in fact it should have been totally absorbing. Am guessing that the visitor centre is now a little more up-to-date than when I visited. Based at Kalgoorlie-Boulder airport, the RFDS continues to 'reach out' to people living in remote areas via the triumvirate of radio, air and medicine. In 2003 the service was (I think) in its 74th year and had grown from the operation of one timber-framed aircraft leased from QANTAS to the large national organisation recognised the world over. It would not be too rash to assume that many hundreds of people owe their lives to the foresight of the founder of the RFDS, the Very Reverend John Flynn.

Next stop, the old mine of Kalgoorlie which, whilst informative, wasn't as good interactively as the Ballarat experience had been. Nevertheless, a further piece of Australian history had been tucked under my belt. What I did though, in true pioneer fashion, was have a go at fossicking with, *yippee*, success. A minuscule speck of gold sat at the bottom of the pan I had been busily swirling water around in, to separate dirt from glitter. It worked! Sadly my prize now seems to have vanished whence it came. But even finding such a microscopic 'nugget' was enough to give me an idea of how the early prospectors must have felt upon striking gold... even a small pocket of gold... surely a giddy rush of gambler's adrenalin?

And then it was off to view the contemporary version of gold extraction, at the largest open cast gold mine in Australia: Super Pit. The name was no mere boast, it was wondrously super-sized. From the viewing area, peering down on dozens of gargantuan earth-moving trucks crawling ant-like up and down the sides of the pit in a sort of orchestrated slo-mo ballet, took on an air of the surreal. The motion never stops. It's as if the scene is on constant replay mode. Colossal as the pit is, they were about to extend it by a further kilometre. An enormous scar on the face of the earth, and sadly no one mentioned the trauma such excavations might cause the indigenous people, whose traditional lands were being eroded on a mega-industrial scale in the necessary name of prosperity. I didn't think to ask, I was too awe-struck by what I was looking at. At the time of my visit, the fact that Kalgoorlie Consolidated Gold Mines worked closely with and supported the local community was not alluded to; but it's good to know that that was the case.

Hopping down from my very small soap box – to continue, my fellow tourists were two elderly couples from Perth, great mates; one couple from Blackpool and one from Cheshire who were, typically, a laugh a minute. There were two girls from Switzerland who spoke (surprisingly) little English (what a hypocrite, I have no second language) and a 'mature' thirty-four year old backpacker from Sweden. He and I had been in the tourist office together the night before so he greeted me like a long-lost friend. My northern chums kept saying, "Your friend's looking for you… your friend's looking out for you… your friend wants you…" etc, etc. Anyway, my 'friend' was horrified when he heard that I was driving on my own down to Esperance and then back west to Perth and lamented the fact that he'd already bought his Greyhound ticket to do roughly the same journey – when he could have travelled with me. "What a pity," I sighed… Today I remain slightly baffled by this exchange…did he volunteer his age? Did I ask him? It's not a question I'd typically start a conversation with. And yet I made no note of his name…

After my Super Pit tour I visited Kalgoorlie's museum and was again drawn to the collection of old photographs; it's the earnest expression on people's faces which draw you in… you so want to know their back-story. In chasing their golden dreams, the miners certainly led a tough existence. Perhaps not quite as tough as the lives led by the pioneers who harvested gum from New Zealand's giant kauri trees, but nevertheless a very harsh existence. Sated by all the information I'd been subjected to in one day, I returned to the hotel where I was duly handed the key to room 212. As I stood outside said room, I thought it unusual for the cleaning staff to leave the television on so late in the day – so I knocked at the door predicting the inevitable outcome – a disgruntled resident. Back downstairs with a jolly, "I didn't know I was sharing…" which fell a bit flat. Swapped keys and was given room 110, so back upstairs I again trundled trusty

George only to find that this room was next to the noisy lift: great!

The evening continued in this vein as I decided to go back to Monty's which turned out to be a bit of a mistake as the glutinous pasta bore not a trace of its Italian ancestry. Perhaps if I had taken the time to think, I would have concluded that steak suited Kalgoorlie's profile better than pasta. Luckily, the hot coffee and cheery service were good on both nights.

The established routine of back to my room after supper continued, and I obediently set about writing up my journal. First though, I phoned home and awoke my slumbering husband with a riddle, "I've just got my first one and you've had lots... what is it?" I won't quote his first answer, but he got there in the end... and then proceeded to reiterate PC Coates' take on the situation. Confession and scribing duties over, feeling drowsy I opted for an early night at which point a very heated discussion erupted between... this sounds like a joke in poor taste, but I assure you it's not... an Australian and a Muslim which got more and more heated as each tried to point out the errors of the other's belief system – unfortunately Islam v. secularism is never an easy (or quiet) mix.

A small wave of depression washed over me as I seemed to be paying all this money for the benefit of another night's lost sleep. *Thank heavens for noisy air-conditioners*, I thought as I twiddled with the controls and at the same moment, I just don't believe it, next door switched on theirs. Fortunately, as the two machines rattled in unison they really did drown out the conversation which was becoming increasingly difficult to ignore.

Sleep at last – well at least until 2am when I awoke absolutely freezing. By now peace reigned up and down the corridor, so I switched off the air conditioner and drifted back to my undisturbed slumbers.

Friday 5th December: a lack of sleep never dents my appetite

My stay at the Plaza might have cut a large lump out of my budget, but I did enjoy my inclusive breakfast. Nothing special really, but just what I wanted: cereal, prunes, yoghurt, fresh fruit, with one slice of squishy toast, grapefruit juice and a cup of Earl Grey. Much better than a 'healthy' snack bar.

Refuelled I hit the road heading south passing through semi-arid terrain to the small mining town of Kambalda, which shed its 1907 gold ghost town status when nickel was discovered in 1954 and the nickel is still being extracted. *Whoa!* Is that a police car I see in my rear view mirror? Don't want to be tailed by the entire Western Australia police force. Alone again and further south, Norseman was the next and last of the goldfields to drive through and marks the point at which the Eyre Highway starts. This is the road which cuts across the Nullabor Plain linking Western Australia to South Australia at Port Augusta just north of Adelaide. I drove for a few kilometers into the Nullabor, for no reason other than to say, "I've driven in the Nullabor"... rather like jumping backwards and forwards over the Tropic of Capricorn... it's there, so you do it.

Norseman is tiny and the now familiar single shop serving all purposes provided a welcome cup of tea and a biscuit. Strolling around this and other similar outlets inevitably provides me with a few minutes of fascination as I inspect the weird array of goods. It must be such a challenge catering for all needs when you are the only shop for miles. The people I meet in these multi-purpose stores are always so friendly and many wear that unmistakable mantle that comes with being a land-worker: weather-beaten and sun-crinkled features. Drifting up and down the aisles, today's selection of items included a light within a three inch high wigwam, cheap electrically-charged versions of pashminas in a variety of day-glo colours (you wouldn't want to shake the hand of someone wearing one) and cans of food which seemed to have been shipped over from Aitutaki and were about to explode. The frozen meat was in carcass sized boxes; this was not a place to ask for "two lamb chops, please"... it was obviously the whole animal or nothing. *Hello!* And what's this? A CD of Winifred Atwell, queen of the boogie-woogie: I made a dusty purchase.

The southerly road continued its way across flat arid land until I at last reached the coast and Esperance, my scheduled night stop. The shoreline is certainly photogenic, so I did the honours pointing the camera first east and then west where, in both directions, receded a handsome line of Norfolk pines. They seem to be made for hanging Christmas baubles on as their branches are so uniform. Esperance Bay is known as the Bay of Isles (granite islands) and it grew in importance as grain from the wheat fields was shipped out in tankers moored alongside 'tanker jetty'. An earlier jetty provided a provisioning point for those working in the eastern goldfields. Today, the town is popular amongst the surfing and scuba diving fraternity – but I think increasingly its shores are patrolled by sleek great whites so, once again with self-preservation in mind, I didn't dabble my toes.

Having strolled up and down the Esperance strand, my watch showed that it was only one-thirty so I decided to push on to Ravensthorpe. Today's scenery has ranged from scrub, to wheat, to one of the most densely populated eucalypt areas in Western Australia, plus the sparkling white sand and aquamarine waters of Esperance. I have seen spring flowers in the more temperate coastal area but, as ever, missed the banksias.

At four o'clock I walked in to the bar of the Palace Hotel, Ravensthorpe, to see if they had a room, and found every bar stool occupied – it's Friday. The occupants turned around as one at my entry which caused a slight pause on my part but the welcome I got was totally cheerful. And yes, a room was available at a reasonable back-packers rate of 49 dollars: that's better!

Two years previously, the census had recorded a population of 344 and I guess the figure for 2003 was fairly similar; it felt as if they were all at the Palace bar when in I walked.

That night I dined on succulent roast chook and veggies, washed down with a cool beer and happily slept like the proverbial. The Palace Hotel had lived up to its imperial name and remains warmly remembered by this itinerant individual.

Saturday 6th December: who's pinched the sun?

Oh dear! Weather not brilliant and it's unexpectedly cold. Travelled via Jerramungup, the Aboriginal word to describe a place of the tall yate tree, the yate being a eucalypt found only in southern Western Australia. Here I stopped for fuel and a slab of banana cake. Dropping crumbs on a rather forlorn forecourt, I reflected that standing at this particular spot really did feel a long way from anywhere. Apart from the tall yate trees, not really aware of anything else of significance. Back on the road, next came the tiny town of Borden with its tiny population of fewer than 200, so it was passed in the blink of an eye. Close to Borden, the landscape begins to open up as the route continues over the Stirling Range. I regret to say that I drove this part of Western Australia's Great Southern region in ignorance of the rare but abundant flora and fauna I was passing. The views and vistas were interrupted by swirling cloud and mist... out of which, unexpectedly, loomed a Dutch windmill. Thinking you don't see too many of these in the southern hemisphere, I stopped for coffee and apple cake and then spent the rest of the day regretting my greed!

Unexpectedly... out of the swirling cloud loomed a Dutch windmill...

Arrived at Albany and visited several of the headlands which make up the dramatic coastline and clambered down to see some (in)active blowholes. Why is it that everything goes to sleep, hibernates, dies early or arrives late when I'm around? On one of my trips I really hope that the whales will be bubble-blowing, the banksias blooming and the blowholes, well, blowing. I drove out along the coast to Discovery Bay to visit Whale World – whaling is considered Australia's first industry as whalers visited Australian shores before settlement and continued their trade well into the 20th century. After settlement, prison ships having discharged their human cargoes, returned to England as whalers. The coastal area around Albany supported bay whaling, as here the whales' migratory route brings them close to the shoreline. In days of whaling, they were harpooned in the bay and hauled straight to the whaling station, where the blubber was removed and rendered down into oil.

So here I was, both fascinated and horrified. Whale World has been established on the site of the Cheynes Beach Whaling Company, which reinvigorated whaling in the area when it began operating in 1952. The work continued until the station's closure in 1978, the last whaling company in Australia to close. It must have been gruesome work, but as with so many grim occupations it bred a closeness and camaraderie amongst the workers and their families. This bond was evident in the photos which adorned the walls of silos which had once held whale oil.

Perhaps I am sounding a little squeamish about Whale World, if so, I am doing the museum an injustice as the information was displayed imaginatively and, despite the desperate subject matter, it was interesting. I find it fascinating learning how people lived and worked over a century ago. It seems as if no settler occupation was without its own set of hazards. Even the men working on the whalers as late as the 1970s weren't exactly enjoying an easy life. Sometimes it's difficult to distance current day understanding of the need to preserve our planet and all who swim, fly and grow on it from the harsh reality of earning a living several decades or centuries ago.

But before I leave, there is an unexpected bonus and I have to investigate. In a large shed I discover a surprising collection of aircraft which had been used as whale spotters, including an historic Catalina flying boat under whose wings the smaller planes were clustered. What a treat!

Sightseeing over for the day, I found a motel in central Albany and booked in for a two day stay. That night I indulged in a two course meal: very unusual… I had obviously forgotten about the double rations of cake.

Sunday 7th December: Albany and its environs

I really warmed to (windy) Albany. In fact, I have warmed to just about everywhere I've visited but after the expanses of open land, here I was looking at expanses of open water. The town appears to run down towards the sea, but in reality Albany came into existence at the landing stage and then slowly expanded up the hill as the population grew. I didn't have any plans for the day, so it made a welcome change to just wander. On a time-limited trip, there is always a pressing desire to see what's over the next hill, but this was the next hill... so here I would stay and look. More Devonshire Cream Tea signs, but after my double-cake extravaganza yesterday, I didn't indulge. No Cornish Cream Teas anywhere. I wonder... did Cornish tin miners travel to Australia to seek their fortunes in the Australian mines? *Aha* – yes they did and they were known as 'Cousin Jacks'. Still don't know why one county's cream tea found favour over another's.

Back to now. Starting by the water, I decided it was time to take in a little of the town's history which, in settlement terms, is a history dating back to Christmas Day 1826. A replica of the Brig *Amity* lies quietly on its moorings, a reminder of Albany's seafaring importance as a strategic deep-water port. It grew in importance ahead of Perth and Fremantle, but eventually suffered a decline when these more northerly ports became established. In 1826 the Brig *Amity* set sail from Sydney bringing a party of soldiers, under the command of Major Edmund Lockyer, and twenty three convicts, the first white settlers to populate Western Australia.

Clustered near the *Amity* are the town's first buildings, including the Old Convict Gaol and Warders quarters. These buildings now house a glitz and glamour-free museum, which, peering into the dark cells, I decided helped to create an idea (a tiny idea) of how tough it would have been for both the prison inmates and the overseer and his family. I imagine the twenty three convicts had not been brought all the way from Sydney to simply occupy prison cells, but instead build them for future generations of miscreants. It is sobering to think that typically those sent from Britain to its penal colonies were guilty of only petty or political crimes, as anything more serious meant dangling from London's Tyburn Tree.

In the overseer's quarters I peered at more sepia photographs and there, to my joy, was a picture of a windmill. The picture was dated circa 1860 and it showed a whitewashed windmill right in the middle of Albany: yesterday's find had not been unique. From the mid-19th-century buildings close to the gaol, a store and convict hiring depot, evolved into accommodation for the government administrator: The Residency. The small community, which started with a gaol, married quarters for officers and little else, was on its way to becoming the town I was looking at today.

For my next bit of sightseeing I drove a little way out of town to the Princess Royal Fortress. Built on a high granite outcrop overlooking the King George Sound, this spot served a strategic purpose. The fortress was officially commissioned in 1893, complete with two gun batteries to protect the bay. Decommissioned in 1956, the guns never fired a shot. In the deep waters of the King George Sound, in 1914 a fleet of troopships gathered to take Australian and New Zealand troops (and horses) to the battle front in Egypt. The troops on board became known as the ANZACS, the first time this nomenclature was attributed.

As the day wore on, the weather improved and the wind, which obviously drove the windmill sails, abated. I was hoping for fair weather tomorrow as an outdoor activity had been planned – the tree top walk up in the lofty branches of the giant karri trees.

Monday 8th December: the Valley of the Giants

The hoped for ongoing weather improvement has not materialised, as I awoke this morning to an even stronger wind and showers. Leaving Albany I bid farewell to the huge grain silo at the edge of the town. Three section road trains bring grain from the wheat fields I'd been driving through, and it's stored in the silo before shipment around the coast of Australia and for export. This is where the giants of the road I had been dodging were headed and it was satisfying to note that Albany is still a thriving port, even if it has been superseded in size by Perth and Fremantle.

Back on the road and undeterred by the elements, am happy to say that the drive to the Valley of the Giants was sublime. The open horizons of the last few days had vanished and it was now time to look at trees. The anticipated giant eucalypts lined the road like aged guards lolling at their duty, but it was disconcerting when bits kept dropping off in the wind. This truly is the land of Tolkien's *Lord of the Rings* Ents, if ever a land of Tolkien's anthropomorphic Ents existed. As light drifted down through the canopy it reflected dramatically off the bark, intensifying the already present folkloric feel. I reiterate: a very, very impressive drive along the South Coast Highway, which took me through the pretty town of Denmark.

On the outskirts of Denmark I stopped for a coffee and was bemused when two weather-beaten, baggy-shorts wearing gentlemen came in and had a head-to-head conflab about what to order. After a lengthy discussion, the first guy looked around the café and finally said, "I'll have a cappuccino." His companion nodded thoughtfully and, with determination, agreed, "So will I." It made me smile, because it seemed such an incongruous choice (probably wouldn't be quite so amusing today). And they so reminded me of Statler and Waldorf, two Muppet characters who first appeared in *Rowan and Martin's Laugh-In*. Odd, that's the second 1960s TV recollection of the week.

Returning to today. Drove a little further west, to an area known as the Walpole Wilderness, where I arrived at the Valley of the Giants Tree Top Walk. To get a better idea of a forested area, nothing beats being up in the canopy. At 40 metres above the ground and 600 metres long, this particular tree top walk is breathtaking – and wobbly but I think it wobbles even on wind-free days. Cleverly, the ascent to the full height is barely discernable as it is so gentle, which makes it fully accessible to all, including wheelchair users. There is also a terra firma walk but the heavens truly opened the moment my feet reached the ground, so I just dashed to say "hello" to the ancient Grandmother Tingle tree which really could have provided the template for the Ent characters. Inspecting her knobbly bark, decided she looked like a benign warty witch.

Buoyed up by today's adventure, I put behind me all bloody memories of whale harpoons and the blubber-covered flensing decks of Albany and set off again on my journey. The tree theme continued as I drove through Franklin Forest, where large swathes were regenerating after a bush-fire, with new tree growth appearing as green fuzz. Heading further west, I drove through the towns of Walpole and Pemberton before finally arriving at Margaret River, where I found a central motel for the night. Explored the busy town and strolled down to the eponymous river where, just over the bridge, sits a bright red steam engine, *Kate*, once used for hauling timber in the Margaret River area and now scrambled over by small children (it's quite a small engine).

Nearby, The Old Settlement represents another 'slice of life' of the settler communities. A cluster of 1920s wooden houses (some of which had been relocated to the spot) and a few pieces of basic farm equipment illustrate lifestyles that would have been in sharp contrast to those lived in the growing urban areas. I had grown used to seeing photographs of wood and corrugated iron dwellings of the 19th century, but these similarly humble abodes were dated rather later. And I complain when I break a fingernail weeding the garden...

Time to potter back to my accommodation.

Tuesday 9th December: Tingle, Tuart and Karri Trees

After days of few trees, I was now surrounded by them. My morning drive had me humming along to the thumping rhythms of Ms Atwell. In contented mood, I decided that this was another beautiful part of the world, the Australian world. The weather during the remainder of my visit was 'temperate' rather than summer sunny weather, but that didn't hamper my enjoyment. I explored the area down to Cape Leeuwin and became totally confused between Tingle, Tuart and Karri trees as I meandered through more forests hunting for the coast. When I drove through Boranup Forest, a sign told me that these were Karri trees. They are unique to this part of the world and are, I think, the tallest hardwood trees in the world growing up to 80 metres. They certainly do soar up into the skies. Some of the tallest specimens have been used as fire-lookouts... and I was squeamish about climbing 30 vertical metres in New Zealand. The climb here is via metal spikes hammered into the tree which spiral upwards. *I'll pass on this if you don't mind.*

At one point, the sun broke through the canopy, transporting me in an instant to a different forest; the light shining through the branches provided a spectacular if spooky light display on the bark of these ancient trees – added to which, and to my joy, a nocturnal possum wandered blearily into view, obviously wondering who had rudely switched on the bright light. There must have been birds flitting in the branches, but alas none flew into view.

Continuing along Cave Road, I realised it had been given that name for a reason. The route I was travelling sits atop the Naturaliste Ridge, a ridge stretching across an extensive calcified sand dune. Water erosion over the millennia has created a honeycomb cluster of over 100 caves of which eight are accessible to the public. With time to visit only one, I chose Lake Cave and was not disappointed. You cannot 'self-guide' but it was no hardship waiting to join the next descent and the numbers weren't too overpowering... and the questions people asked were enthusiastically relevant (always a bonus). The main attraction of this particular cave is the dramatically suspended calcite column which splays out at the bottom like a table top. The column hangs inches above a freshwater lake and at an estimated five tons is one of the world's rarest cave formations. It seems to float weightlessly above the water – it's quite spectacular. The cave is also one of the most active in the area in terms of water dripping and crystals forming. Quite magical and a worthy visit... I drove away feeling blissfully happy and only a little concerned that a sink hole might open up at any moment.

Having emerged from underground, the next stop took me skywards, to the top of Australia's tallest mainland lighthouse: Cape Leeuwin lighthouse. Opened in 1896, this sparkling white edifice still functions guarding one of the world's most treacherous shipping lanes. It now fulfils an additional function as an automatic weather station. Up the steep steps I clambered for a spectacular view across the seas to where the Southern Ocean and Indian Ocean collide. *Wow* – if it's 'mighty windy around Cape Horn', the same can be said for Cape Leeuwin, the most south-westerly tip of Australia. During the months of May to September whales can be spotted on their migratory journey. I was peering out to sea in December.

Elegant Cape Leeuwin lighthouse

Historically, the lighthouse provided a safe passage for ships bound for England, carrying timber from the nearby and then bustling port of Hamelin Bay. For a brief time, access to timber from the colonies provided the necessary material for wooden pavements in Victorian England. The 'Nicolson pavement' lost popularity due to its slippery surface when wet, allowing granite to regain its status as the robust building material of choice. Back down at ground level I went to take a closer look at the sea and found the derelict remains of a calcified water wheel, although the wooden wheel had long since gone. The wheel was erected when a spring was tapped to provide freshwater for the lighthouse construction team and then the keepers. With my back to the lighthouse, I watched two fishermen who were precariously balanced on slippery rocks, casting out to sea, oblivious to the waves which crashed threateningly around their ankles. I hope their seemingly perilous position proved fruitful and not fateful.

With time running out, I didn't drive down to Hamelin Bay to where stingrays are frequently seen, deciding that they would turn and head out to sea the moment I ventured towards the shoreline, so I called it a day and headed back to Margaret River... well, it was getting late.

Wednesday 10th December: an apology to Busselton...

Yesterday I travelled south out of Margaret River to the coast, and now my journey continues its clockwise route, taking me north to Cape Naturaliste and another lighthouse. But before I arrive at the lighthouse, a quick word about what I saw last night...emus strutting across a field – fantastic. Plus, the tally gets better, Western grey kangaroos. Hooray – at last. I saw several on my way back to Margaret River, not exactly large mobs, but enough to stop me feeling despondent about my abysmal wildlife count. Unexpectedly, it was the emus which set my pulse racing... they are big birds.

In a jolly mood, I set off in search of another lighthouse and when I found it, it was not what I was expecting. After the tall elegance of the Cape Leeuwin lighthouse, this stubby version seemed way too small to undertake its designated task. As I approached the Cape Naturaliste beacon I started huffing and puffing. Of course, it was built on a hill sitting atop high ground. The puffing bought back memories of driving through Mundaring 'a high place on a high place'... what a useful name.

Cape Naturaliste lighthouse... seemed way too small
to undertake its designated task

Due to its geographical and geological location, a lighthouse of only 20 metres in height was all that was required to warn passing shipping of the dangerous reefs and currents along this stretch of the coast. Built from local limestone and commissioned in 1904, the original lens is still in use. Nearby the keepers cottages act as a reminder of how isolated the keepers and their families must have felt. Climbing to the top of the lighthouse, I walked the 360 degrees around the balcony looking seaward to the Indian Ocean, then along the magnificent stretch of the Geographe Bay coast, and back across the Leeuwin-Naturaliste National Park. My ponderings about where I had been and where I might be headed were conducted to the *whoomph* of waves breaking down below. My memory is too wonky to recall all the lighthouses I have clambered up, which is a pity, as I should have jotted the names down as an aide-mémoire for my old age.

Next stop on my itinerary was Busselton, where I had planned to spend the night but the town looked, I thought, rather too commercialised. Or perhaps it was just the change of tempo I found unsettling: there were a lot of people... and there hadn't been for the last few days. Feeling I might have done Bussleton an injustice, my research after the event implied that the town was one of Western Australia's favourite tourist spots... what, I wonder, had I missed?

What I hadn't missed, nor could I, was the jetty – which is the major draw to the town, but somehow I didn't register this fact even though I wandered along its length, accompanied by some overly large seagulls. It is the longest wooden jetty in the southern hemisphere stretching almost 2km out to sea. Construction began in 1865 on a more meagre scale, but as the port area became silted and the shipping size increased, the original structure was extended. The last expansion in the 1960s took it to its current length. Once a busy port, the ships docking at Busselton took on board the produce grown in the Wheatbelt area and livestock reared and grazed in the region. The bay also attracted whalers which moored alongside the jetty to take on supplies. In 1972 the jetty was closed to shipping and, without ongoing maintenance, the wooden structure began to fall into disrepair.

In 1978, cyclone Alby caused further destruction and this historic landmark was in danger of total collapse. As is so often the case, a group of dedicated volunteers rallied round and started fundraising to save the historic structure, which, thanks to their efforts has now become a key tourist attraction. The history is fascinating, but the structure didn't lure me like the lighthouses. Okay, if I didn't register the jetty as being a major tourist attraction, I knew I would long remember it for accommodating those large and aggressive seagulls which glared at me with red-rimmed beady eyes. I have no idea what they were thinking, but knew that it was something sinister. For once, food was not involved in this avian stand-off.

... They glared at me with red-rimmed beady eyes...

Bidding farewell to the red-eyed gulls, on I went to Mandurah. Arriving at my destination at about six in the evening, it was therefore beer time... which I glugged down overlooking the Peel-Harvey estuary. The harbour is larger than Sydney's and having turned a geographical corner I had moved out of a temperate zone into a balmy Mediterranean one: the ideal climate for supping ale beside the sea.

Accommodation proved a bit of a challenge, but I eventually found a room at the Foreshore Motel... which wasn't on the foreshore. It's odd what appeals and what doesn't, because this was truly basic but I really loved my sea-blue room. Yes, it had seen better days but I felt quite snug possibly because the door stuck so fast that you had to heft it open with your shoulder and repeat the action, in reverse, to close it.

Having mastered the art of ingress and egress, I celebrated by taking myself out for a stroll and an evening meal. Perhaps peopled places have their good points.

Thursday 11th December: Short journal entries…

… which I don't think should be interpreted as traveller fatigue, more likely to be writer fatigue as my entries fizzle out between Mandurah and Perth. I hadn't quite blown in from the back of beyond, but where a day or so ago I had been gazing at tingles and tuarts, now I was negotiating traffic and surrounded by buildings. Where once there had been wheat-fields in my line of vision, now there was a ribbon of development running northwards towards Perth. And as soon as I reached Fremantle, I had seen it before.

The only words I did jot down today were: 'Trip up the Murray River – accompanied by a small pod of dolphins.'

I regret I can't embellish this scanty record.

Friday 12th December: Perth is in my sights, via…

Rockingham and Fremantle, where I visit the excellent Shipwrecks Museum…

Again, the brevity of the note begs an explanation… but none is forthcoming. We could both, you and I, Google the Shipwrecks Museum, but that would seem like cheating. All I can assume is that 'excellent' is the correct adjective and leave it at that.

Back in the city, I had to intentionally part with the Commodore and to unintentionally part with Winifred Atwell (would I ever have played her again?)

With 3057km clocked up (which translates to just 100 short of 2,000 miles) I felt quite emotional that another road odyssey was over, so cheered myself up with a carrot, ginger, celery and apple juice, my favourite pick-me-up concoction.

Successfully negotiating the steps, George and I received a "Welcome back to Sullivans Hotel" from a beaming receptionist and I said a familiar "hello again" to their much used, much needed laundry room.

Saturday 13th December: day at leisure

Five days to go before I head over to Sydney, but today I am just going to wander around this lovely city and relax before I get ready for tomorrow's trip to Broome. Met a couple at breakfast from East Wittering, a town close to my English home: small world!

Pottering back into the centre of Perth, I strolled past a beauty parlour and had one of those bizarre 'well, why not?' moments. After the dust of the last few days, the perfumed air of the salon seemed inviting (had I already forgotten the heady eucalypt-laden air of the Margaret River area?) So in I went to have a relaxing facial, which relaxed me for all of ten minutes before I had my eyelashes tinted. *Why?* I had never had them tinted before. They're short, sparse and hardly worth spending money on. But I did – and I won't be having them tinted again. I don't suffer from claustrophobia, but lying back being told not to open your eyes… under any circumstances… whilst you listen to doors softly opening and closing and hear voices whispering…well, it's strangely unnerving. I could feel sweat trickling down my cleavage as I sat trapped in a plastic chair and unable to see what was happening around me. There was nothing relaxing about this experience. And it undid all the good work of the facial. As makeovers go, that's as extreme as I ever want to experience. *Brrr…*

Treatment over, I paid and scuttled out faster than a scuttling centipede, and sought solace in a cup of coffee. Dashing into the coffee shop loo, I peered in the mirror where two red-rimmed eyes blinked back at me. The Busselton gulls would have welcomed me as one of their own. Sexily batting my eyelashes at my reflection in an imagined 'come-hither' fashion, I realised that they looked not one jot different from their appearance at breakfast. What an experience. Not to be repeated… but at least it wasn't a tattoo… actually, perhaps a tiny one would have been more exciting. I'm sure the tattoo artists have seen wobbly skin before. *Next time…?*

Broome and Derby

Sunday 14th December to Wednesday 17th December: remote places I just had to see

The following morning, I made a bleary eyed return to Perth airport for a flight north to Broome, back to the land of red sand. Arriving at tiny Broome airport I knew it had been a good decision to tack on this extra trip: I had come so far and seen so much, but this I felt certain would be utterly different. I made my way to the Seashells Resort, where I stayed for four nights. I think the very small swimming pool made it a 'resort'. On checking in, I was a little bit alarmed when the receptionist cheerily told me about a break-in that had recently taken place in one of the rooms, even though the patio door through which the man had entered had been firmly locked shut. "Thank you" I said and after that spent four fairly sleepless nights in a room lit up like Blackpool.

Now Broome is another of the world's laid-back, flip-flop destinations so, unsurprisingly, much time was spent flip-flopping around and swimming. Admittedly all this idleness was interspersed with activity. However, to reduce the tedium of describing yet another wallow in glorious water, I have lumped together the more journalistic highlights... beginning with...

... a sunset camel trek along Cable Beach – I know it's a very touristy thing to do, but I really enjoy sitting on top of a disdainful dromedary as it lurches along rhythmically, giving its passenger a sort of pilates workout as you sway in time to its steady footfall. Unfortunately, feral camels are a bit of a problem, so perhaps a life spent plodding up and down a sandy beach with tourists on your back is better than being hunted down for meat. They are also good water diviners, but I guess only a few beasts are lucky enough to be 'hired' for that particular skill. The white sand of Cable Beach stretches for 22km and is washed clean every day by Broome's crystal clear tides, which rise up to ten metres at a time. As described, Broome is truly a laid-back flip-flop sort of place, and what else could it be with all that sandy loveliness?

... A touristy thing to do...

Not far from Broome, in the Kimberley Waterways, saltie crocodiles make their home. Several years ago, a professional hunter and documentary-maker turned conservationist, Malcolm Douglas, rescued half a dozen large prehistoric beasts from the waterways and opened his crocodile park. I paid the park a visit and stood behind some rusty fencing looking at some enormous saltie specimens. A large beast lunged at the fence, seemingly without provocation... which caused the assembled onlookers, me included, to leap backwards as one. The crocs are also farmed... and I had a bit of a problem with that and still do, although I have eaten and enjoyed crocodile meat: a moral conundrum. Since the demise of its founder, the park has since been relocated and has expanded to become the Malcolm Douglas Wilderness Wildlife Park.

Pre the days of tourists in the 1880s, Broome had been Western Australia's most profitable pearling region, with divers from Asia undertaking the dangerous work of retrieving the pearl-bearing oysters. Broome still maintains its multicultural legacy with the presence of original shops and stores run by successive generations descended from the 19th-century pearl divers and the communities that they established. I strolled around China Town and visited the Chinese and Japanese cemeteries, where the many hundreds of pearl diver graves bore testament to the danger of their work.

Continuing the pearl theme, I hired a small red 4WD (all hire cars seem to be red) and drove out to Willie Creek Pearl Farm which is 38km north of Broome. The track down to the farm is red-rutted sand, like corrugated iron, and I was a little concerned that my lovely little 4WD might protest, but it bounced along happily. The tidal flats provide the perfect environment for farmed oysters and cultured pearls: the pearls take between two and three years to grow. The pearl farm arranges tours which include setting out in a teeny weeny tin boat to inspect the oyster beds. I thoroughly enjoyed my visit, but it was *so* hot: a dry heat unlike the Darwin heat.

On another day, I drove 220km further north to the remote town of Derby, which is famed for being the gateway to the Windjana Gorge and the Gibb River Road – areas it's probably best to explore in company. The 700km Gibb River Road runs from Derby through the Kimberley Plateau up to the northern coast at Cambridge Gulf. Built originally as a cattle route, the road draws intrepid tourists keen to explore one of the more isolated regions of Australia. Planning, timing and stamina are fundamental to enjoying a safe journey. Hazards include the route being liable to flooding in the wet season and the surface is mainly sandy dirt, much of it corrugated, and gravel. Having tackled approximately 60kms of this juddering terrain on my pearl trip, I can confirm that corrugated surfaces are not good if you suffer from a bad back... and are possibly liable to give you one if you don't.

Driving into Derby, I proceeded to drive the wrong way down the town's very public dual carriage way. Surely this town was way too small for such traffic sophistication but no one seemed at all bothered by my decision to ignore the road signs. The one main road leads right down to the water... and that's the second of Derby's claims to fame. Unlike Broome, the tidal difference here can exceed a staggering 12 metres and the six hourly surge of water is joined by the silty outflow of the Fitzroy River – which explained the very muddy mud flats I was standing looking at. I had driven all this way to gaze across gloppy mud. And I didn't even see a mud crab or crocodile, both of which patrol the area. Predictably, I did venture for a kilometre or two along the Gibb River Road: result!

On the journey up from Broome, I had stopped to photograph the 1,000–1,500-year-old Prison Boab tree, all of fourteen metres in circumference. At the end of the 19th century, the hollow trunk was used to house prisoners overnight before they walked the final part of their journey into Derby. Today it is a sacred Aboriginal site (well I guess it was in the 19th century and way before that).

On my journey back down to Broome, I felt as if I was in the American mid-west being chased by a twister. Bowling merrily along I became aware of a drop in the light level and just glanced skywards – nothing up a head, but a peek over my shoulder revealed that I was being chased by storm clouds – large threatening grey skyscraper versions. The memory of them bearing down on me still provokes a small mental shudder. I was happily driving through remote sandy nothingness and hadn't been paying attention to the dipping fuel gauge, and when I did notice the dial tickling empty – there seemed to be no sign of human life anywhere, just me and those towering clouds for company. Glancing in my rear view mirror the clouds appeared to grow in a way that I only thought possible when looking at a film played at double-speed. The clouds moved menacingly from behind to beside me, they seemed within touching distance but realistically must have been a few miles over to my left. The way they seemed to sweep the ground as they advanced, was heart-poundingly spectacular.

Just as I was beginning to wonder how strong the accompanying wind might be when joy of joys, I arrived at a petrol station sitting all alone apart from an array of rickety outbuildings. As I pulled up I noticed that everything was painted green – the buildings, the pumps, the few tables and chairs, and the guy who came out to greet me was clad in green overalls. I felt as if I'd strayed on to a David Lynch film set. If I was surprised to see a petrol station, and a unique one at that, the overalled chap didn't seem too startled to see lone me. His small talk stretched no further than guessing my destination and asking if I'd like some tea. He filled up the car's obviously small tank whilst I took shelter with a mug of (non-green) tea and watched as the storm swept swiftly and majestically on its way. When my 'hero' announced that the storm had passed, I continued my journey… thankfully and uneventfully.

Moral of the tale, in order to maintain an even blood pressure, keep an eye on the fuel gauge and fill up sooner rather than later. And remember, small vehicles usually have small petrol tanks. Not the sort of mistakes to make for someone who is toying with the idea of returning one day to drive the Gibb River Road.

Safely back at Seashells Resort, I reflected that although my time in Broome and Derby had been relatively short, I had found this stretch of the Western Australian coastline hypnotically beguiling and as anticipated, 'utterly different'. It is hard to put into words the appeal of immense stretches of sandy nothingness but it seems so appropriate and right that an oyster should take a grain of that sand and turn it into a pearl. Although, after my trip to Willie Creek I think the grain of sand in a cultured pearl is something of a romantic misnomer, but an invading technician with a manufactured bead or a bit of muscle shell, doesn't quite conjure up images of Bizet's *The Pearl Fishers*.

Now the big question… will I ever again stand on that little piece of Australian coastline? I would so like to think that one day I might return. I feel certain that whatever happens, I will always hear the beckoning call of Broome's gentle lapping waves and want to dabble my toes one more time. It was the perfect place to end my solo, but somehow never alone, travels. Nothing I had done had been overly dramatic, but it had all been wonderful and was certainly my very own adventure.

Journey's End

Thursday 18th December: back down to Perth and off to Sydney

My last solo day was entirely taken up with flying, first down to Perth and then after a couple of hours lolling around Perth airport with little to do it was off to Sydney where I was reunited with my family in time for Christmas – an emotional ending to a really wonderful Top End and Western Australia trip.

I think I have now joined up many of the major dots linking the cities and iconic sights, which are scattered around and across Australia. Of course, there is still much more to see and experience in this enormous and diverse country but I feel privileged to have experienced as much as I have. Inspired by all that I have learnt about the oral traditions of the indigenous people, should the opportunity to undertake another Australian journey ever arise, I would certainly view the landscape through more enlightened eyes. Queensland and the Daintree Rainforest beckon... so who knows?

That is the future, but reflecting on what I did and what I saw, nothing can detract from, nor diminish, the impact of the wonderful time I had in all of the countries that I visited. It is impossible to thank those characters who drifted across my path and told me snippets of their stories. I'm not sure that I gave back much in return, except perhaps a listening ear and the occasional stifled yawn.

And I drove all those miles without giving a thought to what might happen if I needed to change a car tyre. From memory, I could probably tackle a tyre on one of Peter Briggs' MGs, but a Holden V6 Commodore... that I very much doubt. Luckily, I wasn't put to the test.

Finally, as a message to all those mums and dads whose children have headed off to pastures new, smash the piggy bank, pack your own 'George' and go and have an adventure. It's your turn now.

Hello Sydney... reunited with my family in time for Christmas

Acknowledgements

I am indebted to Tim Beer for his fun and quirky illustrations which add a lively dimension to the text. After a fulfilling career as a Rheumatologist, Tim now devotes his time to painting and sculpture. As the 'fatalistic' father of my adored daughter-in-law, Alice, he needed little persuading to swap paint brush and clay for sharpened pencil. In this ideal medium he captured some of the weird and wonderful moments of my trip to see how our offspring were faring. Tim's more typical work can be viewed at *timcbeer.co.uk*

In addition, I would like to thank the various organisations, whose publications, attractions and activities kept me informed and entertained, for allowing me to include extracts from their promotional literature in the body of the book's text. And especially I would like to thank Footprint Travel Guides, Trailfinders and Waitomo Adventures for their kind words of encouragement which eased my furrowed-brow and were greatly appreciated: I hope the memories of my 'mission' will not disappoint.

And I owe a personal "thank you" to family, friends and the team at The Book Guild:

To Kevin, Matt, Alice and Kate – without you I would be spending my retirement flicking a duster and re-arranging ornaments. "Thank you" doesn't do it justice!

To Anne Herbert, Christine Hicks and Stephanie Spink – how lucky am I to have friends like you! You all believed in George when I wavered with a timid "really…"

To the Heyshott Book Club, who cheered me on with a glass or two of vino and much laughter and only occasionally quizzed "how long…" to write a book.

Last but not least, to Jeremy Thompson and his enthusiastic team at The Book Guild: Philippa Iliffe, Hannah Virk, Jack Wedgbury and Katherine Ward. Without your imagination and support George's travels would have come to an abrupt and inglorious end.

Thank you one and all.

Web Addresses

The following web addresses are current but I stress that they relate to attractions and venues I visited in 2002 and 2003 so aspects of the places I mention may have changed.

Australia

Canberra
Parliament House, Canberra: www.aph.gov.au

New South Wales
Bridge Climb, Sydney Harbour: www.bridgeclimb.com
Snowy Mountains Scheme: www.environment.nsw.gov.au

Northern Territory
Adelaide River War Cemetery: www.adelaideriver-warcemetery.
    australianwarheroes.com
Bowali Visitor Centre: www.kakadunationalparkaustralia.com
Uluru Cultural Centre: https://parksaustralia.gov.au
Window on the Wetlands Visitor Centre: www.nt.gov.au

South Australia
Art Gallery of South Australia: www.artgallery.sa.gov.au
Mount Gambier: https://mountgambier.sa.gov.au
National Motor Museum, Birdwood: www.motor.history.sa.gov.au
South Australia Museum: www.samuseum.sa.gov.au

Victoria
Cape Otway Lightstation: www.lightstation.com
Old Melbourne Gaol: www.oldmelbournegaol.com.au
Sovereign Hill, Ballarat: www.sovereignhill.com.au
Split Point Lighthouse: www.splitpointlighthouse.com.au

Western Australia
Art Gallery of Western Australia: www.artgallery.wa.gov.au
Brig Amity and Old Convict Gaol, Albany: www.albany.asn.au
Cape Leeuwin Lighthouse: www.lighthouses.org.au
Cape Naturaliste Lighthouse: www.lighthouses.org.au
Malcolm Douglas Wilderness Wildlife Park: www.malcolmdouglas.com.au
Old Settlement, Margaret River: www.workinglife.com.au/margaret-river-old-settlement
Princess Royal Fortress: www.albanyregion.com.au
Royal Flying Doctor Service: www.flyingdoctor.org.au/wa
Shipwrecks Museum, Fremantle: www.museum.wa.gov.au
Swan Bells Bell Tower: www.swanbells.com.au
Valley of the Giants Tree Top Walk: www.valleyofthegiants.com.au
Whale World, Discovery Bay: www.discoverybay.com.au
Willie Creek Pearl Farm: www.williecreekpearlfarm.com.au
York Courthouse Complex: www.nationaltrust.org.au
York Motor Museum: www.yorkmotormuseum.com

Cook Islands
Cook Islands Museum: www.cook-islands-library-museum.org

Kuala Lumpur
Lake Park: www.klbotanicalgarden.gov.my
National Museum: www.kuala-lumpur.ws/attractions/national-museum
Petronas Towers: www.petronastwintowers.com.my

Los Angeles
The Getty Center: www.getty.edu

North Island New Zealand
Dargaville Maritime Museum: www.dargavillemuseum.co.nz
Discover Waitomo: www.waitomo.com
Kauri Museum, Matakohe: www.kau.nz
Kerikeri Mission House: www.heritage.org.nz
Otorohanga Kiwi House: www.kiwihouse.org.nz
Russell Museum: www.russellmuseum.org.nz
Wai-o-tapu Thermal area: www.waiotapu.co.nz
Waitangi Treaty Grounds & Museum: www.waitangi.org.nz
Waitomo Adventures Ltd: www.waitomo.co.nz

Endnotes

1   Ashley, Clifford A, The Yankee Whaler (USA: Dover Maritime, 2014) p.114

2   The Kauri Museum, http://www.kau.nz

3   Waitomo Adventures Ltd Information Sheet, http://www.waitomo.co.nz

4   The Old Melbourne Gaol, www.oldmelbournegaol.com.au

5   O'Brien, Katrina and Andrew Swaffer, Footprint West Coast
    Australia Handbook (Bath: Footprint Handbooks Ltd, 2003)
    p.129, www.footprinttravelguides.com